EMPLOYMENT LAW SIMULATIONS

Aïda M. Alaka
Washburn University School of Law

BRIDGE TO PRACTICE SERIES®

Bridge to Practice Series® is a trademark registered in the U.S. Patent and Trademark Office.

© 2020 LEG, Inc. d/b/a West Academic
    444 Cedar Street, Suite 700
    St. Paul, MN 55101
    1-877-888-1330

West, West Academic Publishing, and West Academic are trademarks of West Publishing Corporation, used under license.

Printed in the United States of America

ISBN: 978-1-64020-811-7

For my husband
John Rury

PREFACE

There is a growing need within the legal profession for law students to graduate "practice ready" such that they possess competence in the fundamental skills and values of the profession. While many law schools have added experiential learning opportunities to meet this need, most students need multiple opportunities to practice and assess their lawyering skills to be ready to practice effectively upon graduation. This book provides several opportunities for you to do just that.

Regardless of whether you enter the profession as a sole practitioner or as a member of a large law firm, law practice requires many competencies: problem-solving, legal analysis and reasoning, legal research, fact investigation, communication, counseling, and negotiation skills, among others.[1] Additionally, lawyers should be committed to promoting justice, fairness, and their own professional self-development.

Studies[2] suggest that budding professionals should traverse the following three conceptual apprenticeships to develop their abilities within these domains:

1. **Knowledge:** the intellectual or cognitive apprenticeship that "focuses the student on the knowledge and way of thinking of the profession" in the context of the relevant subject matter;[3]

2. **Practice:** the apprenticeship that focuses on developing the ability and particular skills required for the practice of the profession;[4]

3. **Professionalism:** the apprenticeship that focuses on the purposes, attitudes, and values of the professional community.[5]

Taken together, these three apprenticeships constitute the process of professional formation through which emerging lawyers develop professional identities necessary to shoulder the significant responsibilities to those they serve. Focusing on these apprenticeships during law school allows students to assess their own development as they proceed through their courses.

Drawing on the apprenticeship model, this book contains problems designed to help you develop the professional skills necessary for your success. Thus, you will be able to assess your competence and increase your confidence in:

- Finding, analyzing, and applying the multiple layers of federal, state, and local laws affecting the employment relationship;

- Researching, drafting, counseling, and other skills required in an employment-law practice; and

- Understanding the professional boundaries that will guide your role in the prosecution or defense of employment-law claims.

Although the problems are set in the context of employment law, the knowledge, skills, and values that are emphasized in this book will be useful in any law-practice context. Thus, regardless

---

[1] ROBERT MACCRATE ET AL., LEGAL EDUCATION AND PROFESSIONAL DEVELOPMENT—AN EDUCATIONAL CONTINUUM 138–41 (1992) (listing the Fundamental Lawyering Skills identified by the Taskforce on Law Schools and the Profession).

[2] *See, e.g.,* WILLIAM M. SULLIVAN ET AL., EDUCATING LAWYERS: PREPARATION FOR THE PROFESSION OF LAW 25–46 (2007); Judith Welch Wegner, *The Carnegie Foundation's* Educating Lawyers: *Four Questions for Bar Examiners,* BAR EXAMINER, June 2011, at 11.

[3] SULLIVAN, *supra* note 2, at 28.

[4] *See id.*

[5] *Id.*

of whether you ultimately practice employment law, the goal of this book is to assist you in constructing a strong bridge from law school to law practice. Enjoy!

AMA

ACKNOWLEDGMENTS

I have long considered writing a practice-oriented employment-law text so other instructors might benefit from exercises I developed for my own employment law course. No book is written alone, however, and this is no exception. I have many people to thank in seeing my somewhat vague idea take shape and come to fruition.

First, I thank my colleague, Joseph Mastrosimone, for helping me conceptualize the text. We had hoped to undertake the project together, but administrative duties stood in the way of that collaboration. Nonetheless, I owe Joe a great deal of gratitude for providing insights from his own law practice, helping to develop research problems that inspired some of my exercises, and simply encouraging me and providing invaluable feedback along the way.

I was also assisted by two Washburn Law librarians, Barbara Ginzburg and Creighton Miller. Over the years, they have identified resources that deepen the state-law dimension in my courses, and thus contributed to this book.

My research assistants, Washburn Law students Claire Hillman and Dean Kirk, undertook the task of verifying research results, cite-checking, and formatting footnotes. I appreciate their care and professionalism in approaching this somewhat thankless task.

This project may not have been finalized without the expertise of Washburn Law student, Rachel Schwein. I could not have had a better partner in editing, merging, and formatting the many individual documents that contributed to the text. I am also grateful for Mona Alaka's expert assistance in reviewing and providing feedback on my finished draft.

I would also like to thank the many Washburn employment law students who conducted many of the research exercises and presented their findings in class. Their feedback over the years confirmed the idea that combining doctrine with practice in a traditional case-book course can yield valuable lessons.

Finally, I would like to thank my husband, John Rury. Without his mentorship and support, I could not have made the transition from law practice to the academy. His dedication to his own writing and scholarly career over the years has been inspiring. For all that he does, I dedicate this book to him.

SUMMARY OF CONTENTS

TABLE OF CONTENTS

EMPLOYMENT LAW SIMULATIONS

CHAPTER ONE

INTRODUCTION TO LAW PRACTICE

I. INTRODUCTION

This chapter addresses three separate and seemingly unconnected topics: billing time, researching the law, and establishing the client relationship. What connects these topics are their importance to the successful transition from student to law practice and the insecurity that many new lawyers feel about their ability to perform these essential tasks.

This chapter also introduces students to Daisy Depot, one of the companies that will figure prominently in this book. As in law practice, it will not be the only company students will represent or oppose, but employment lawyers often encounter a company more than once—whether as clients or opponents. One of the many skills necessary to be an effective counselor or litigator is becoming an expert on the client as well as the law. Learning about new and interesting industries is one of the many benefits of an employment-law practice.

A. BILLING TIME

In many law-practice settings, including government and corporate in-house departments, revenue is not generated specifically based on the attorney's labor. For lawyers engaged in private practice, however, the continued viability of their firms is dependent on compensation for the legal work performed. Thus, an attorney's value is often measured by billable hours or the revenue generated by her time and efforts—either through direct client billing, fee shifting, or contingent fee arrangements.

Clear, timely, accurate, and ethical timekeeping is indispensable for lawyers whose labor is tied to revenue generation. Unclear, inaccurate, and unethical billing practices are the subject of "jokes," as well as scholarly[1] and practice-oriented articles[2] and books,[3] and, most importantly, complaints to bar authorities. At a minimum, ethical and timely billing practices keep the lights on.

Billing time requires tracking time and activities to particular clients and to particular "matters" or "cases." Attorneys, and the law firms in which they work, often handle more than one matter for a client. For example, a firm could represent the same client in a merger, a contract dispute with a supplier, a discrimination claim with a former employee, and an environmental clean-up case. Labor and employment counsel may review employment handbooks, provide counsel on the risks involved in disciplining a problematic employee, represent the client in litigation, or conduct compliance training or evaluation.

In most cases, all of these activities must be separately identified and tracked to a billable "matter." Depending on the billing arrangement the firm has with the client, it could be insufficient to consolidate all time. Thus, you would probably need to identify more than the client name and activity you are billing for; instead, you would need to identify the client name, matter, (e.g. "plant

---

[1] *E.g.*, Lisa G. Lerman, *Regulation of Unethical Billing Practices: Progress and Prospects*, 1998 PROF. LAW. SYMP. ISSUES 89 (1998).

[2] A simple "google" search will reveal many articles and blog posts on attorney billing practices. *See, e.g.*, Diane Karpman, *Make sure billing practices are bulletproof*, CAL. B.J. (Dec. 2013), http://www.calbarjournal.com/December2013/EthicsByte; Megan Zavieh, *Billing to Avoid Ethics Complaints*, LAWYERIST (Apr. 30, 2013), https://lawyerist.com/blog/billing-to-avoid-ethics-complaints/; Nicole Black, *Things You Didn't Learn in Law School: Billing*, MYCASE (Oct. 2013), https://www.mycase.com/blog/2013/10/things-didnt-learn-law-school-billing/.

[3] *E.g.,* WILLIAM G. ROSS, THE HONEST HOUR: THE ETHICS OF TIME-BASED BILLING BY ATTORNEYS (Carolina Academic Press 1996).

closing"), and activity. Even when clients are charged on a project basis, rather than an hourly basis, having an accurate record of your activities is indispensable to ensure that future arrangements are profitable.

The exercises in this book will require you to engage in many typical law-practice activities, including researching, drafting, interviewing, and counseling. Take the opportunity to keep meticulous track of those activities. Learning best practices now will ease your transition from law school to practice.

CLIENT AND MATTER NUMBERS

Billing codes vary from firm to firm, but they should be clear, straightforward, and informational. Below is a set of example descriptions and matter numbers a firm might use for the client Daisy Depot.

Description	Client	Matter Numbers
Daisy Depot General Counseling	DD	GC0001
Daisy Depot Child Labor Research: Wages & Hours	DD	CLR001
Daisy Depot Child Labor Research: Occupations	DD	CLR002

TIME-KEEPING CODES

When billing time, referencing the client and matter numbers or codes is not enough. Clients, and in some cases the courts, will want to see the detail of what an attorney was doing to justify the bill. The American Bar Association's Litigation Section has developed a uniform task-based management system for litigation-related billing, which provides an excellent overview of the litigator's billable tasks, fees, and costs, and serves as a guide for keeping track of billable activities.[4] While these codes are an important source of information, you can use the following simple conventions to record your time throughout the course unless your professor instructs otherwise.

TASK BASED BILLING SYSTEM

Activity	Abbreviation	Other Information to Include
Researching a particular issue or point of law	Res re:	Identify issue or point of law
Review document(s)/law	Rev	Identify document(s) or law
Draft a document	Draft	Identify document
Revise a document	Rvs	Identify document
Plan and prepare for	PPF	Identify activity
Communicate with	Comm w/ [ ] re [ ]	Identify individual(s) and subject of the communication
Attend meeting	Attend mtg w/ [ ] re [ ]	Identify individual(s) and subject of the meeting
Other abbreviations as necessary as long as they make sense to the average reader		

---

[4] *Litigation Code Set*, A.B.A. (rev. June 8, 2018), https://www.americanbar.org/groups/litigation/resources/uniform_task_based_management_system/litigation_code_set/.

TIME-KEEPING TIPS

- Record and bill *all time* spent on each project. This includes time spent researching, writing, and meeting with others.
- You may use abbreviations when describing your activities but be specific and clear.
- You may refer to your teammates or other individuals by their first initial and last name; J. Smith, for example.
- Time submitted for the month should be totaled.

EXAMPLE

Date	Client/Matter	Activity Description	Hours
9/22/20	DD:CLR 001	Rev letter from P. Duquette re child labor audit; Res re: permissible working hours/school days.	1.2
9/22/20	AA:JM 001	Attend mtg. w/ Q. Smith, A. Patel, & L. Zuaiter re mediation prep.	2.8
9/22/20	DD:CLR 002	Draft chart re hazardous orders.	1.4
9/23/20	DD:CLR 001	Res re: permissible working hours/summer; disc. w/ P. Duquette re same; beg. drafting letter to DOL.	4.4
TOTAL			9.8

B. RESEARCHING EMPLOYMENT LAW

Legal practice requires the ability to find, read, analyze, communicate, and use the law on behalf of one's client. While most law school courses will help you to develop your ability to read and analyze the law, few courses after your first year will require you to find, communicate, and use the law in a lawyering context. Casebook-oriented courses may unintentionally diminish the importance of acquiring these foundational skills because they largely focus on appellate cases in which lawyers have presumably found the relevant law.

The ability to conduct legal research includes key fundamental skills:

1. Knowing the nature of legal rules and institutions, including the sources of legal rules and the processes by which they are made;

2. Knowing and being able to use fundamental tools of legal research, including where to find primary and secondary legal texts and the ethical rules of the profession;

3. Possessing specialized techniques for reading and using primary legal texts;

4. Possessing familiarity with secondary legal resources and the ability to judge their value; and

5. The ability to plan and implement a coherent and effective research design.[5]

It can be easy to view legal research as a task-based skill; that is, to focus on the activity of researching. Doing so misses the fact that "the resolution of legal problems [is] an iterative and analytical process"[6] that involves all three of the apprenticeships referred to in the preface to this book: knowledge, practice, and professionalism. Analyzing research competency under the apprenticeship framework, legal research professionals have found that you, as a student, will

---

[5]   *See* ROBERT MACCRATE ET AL., LEGAL EDUCATION AND PROFESSIONAL DEVELOPMENT—AN EDUCATIONAL CONTINUUM 31–34 (1992).

[6]   SUSAN NEVELOW MART, THE BOULDER STATEMENTS ON LEGAL RESEARCH EDUCATION: THE INTERSECTION OF INTELLECTUAL AND PRACTICAL SKILLS 250 (William S. Hein & Co. ed., 2014).

experience the first apprenticeship, the *cognitive* apprenticeship, "by learning the importance of understanding the legal system in which [your] question arises and evaluating the available legal resources."[7] Moreover, you will "synthesize information about legal systems and resources to identify the best research plan for a given question."[8] Achieving competence as a legal researcher also means you must continuously reevaluate your reliance on particular law as new facts about a client's matter emerge; new facts may implicate different controlling law.[9] It also means internalizing the need to consult secondary sources to get an overview of unfamiliar areas of law and to understand the larger context in which the law operates.

This cognitive process is particularly important in employment law, which is governed by an "alphabet soup" of federal, state, and local laws, each of which could determine the outcome of a particular legal query. Additionally, employment-law practitioners must consider how the laws apply at various points in the employment relationship. The research problems throughout this book are designed to assist you in developing mental checklists during the research process to account for these variables.

Identifying material facts, determining legal issues, and locating, evaluating, and using research authorities marry the cognitive apprenticeship with the *practical* one,[10] the second apprenticeship. While you may be adept at finding resources though Westlaw or Lexis, the ability to quickly locate a variety of publicly available resources is also imperative, particularly for those of you who will work in practice environments without ready access to subscription resources. Many of the problems in this book will facilitate this skill by familiarizing you with government websites containing relevant law and guidance.

The ability to conduct comprehensive research is also part of a lawyer's ethical and professional responsibilities.[11] Missing or misunderstanding outcome-determinative legal principles can significantly affect your career and your clients' interests. To engage the final apprenticeship, the *professional* apprenticeship, the research problems ask you to assume the role of a lawyer engaged in research to advise a client. You should use this opportunity to internalize your professional and ethical responsibilities and to experience the professional boundaries that will guide your role in the prosecution and defense of employment claims. Because the laws and agency rules governing the rights and obligations of employers and employees are particularly susceptible to political changes, research skills coupled with attention to employment-law news and analysis are critically important to maintaining professionalism.

In the heavily regulated area of employment law, practitioners must understand the importance of the federal and state agencies that regulate the relationship between employees and employers. These agencies are not only excellent resources for finding law or guidance on many different topics but, in their enforcement capacity, agencies also investigate alleged violations of the laws they regulate. By publishing general information, frequently asked questions, interpretive guidance, and links to current laws and regulations, agencies provide an important source of information for attorneys, workers, and employers alike.

---

[7] *Id.*

[8] *Id.*

[9] Research competency also includes the ability to master a variety of research resources. Reliance on one database alone can preclude one from obtaining the most relevant results in a digital search. *See* Susan Nevelow Mart, *Results May Vary*, A.B.A. J., Mar. 2018, at 48, http://scholar.law.colorado.edu/articles/964/.

[10] *See id.*

[11] *See id.* A recent survey of over 100 federal and state judges revealed that litigants missed important cases and other relevant precedent with important negative consequences for the litigation. *See* Jake Heller, *You're Bad at Legal Research, and Your Judge Knows It*, ABOVE THE LAW (May 24, 2018, 2:34 P.M.), https://abovethelaw.com/2018/05/artificial-confusion-youre-bad-at-legal-research-and-your-judge-knows-it/.

Inexperienced practitioners often jump directly to case law without looking first for controlling statutes or doing general background research. Doing so risks many critical errors, including:

1. Failing to understand the larger context in which the legal issues arise;

2. Failing to understand how multiple sources of law intersect in a particular situation;

3. Failing to consider whether a case is addressing current law, including any amendments to the law;

4. Failing to recognize that a statute doesn't apply, because, for example, the corporate client is not an "employer" under the act;

5. Failing to understand that a case is not necessarily applicable, even when the facts of the case are substantially similar to the client's case; and

6. Failing to find important exemptions located in other sections of the act.

When addressing questions that are controlled by the application of statutory law, it is important to (1) start with the text of the statute, including any definitions, (2) determine whether any regulations or guidance documents address the operative provisions of the statute, and (3) determine whether any controlling precedent interprets the statute or the regulations.

The most important federal agencies for employment lawyers are the Equal Employment Opportunity Commission (eeoc.gov) and Department of Labor (dol.gov), as well as the state departments of labor and fair employment practices agencies (FEPAs) in the states in which they practice. You should take some time to explore the federal websites and those of your own states before commencing research for the following problems in this book. Understanding what information can be obtained from the agencies now can save time and trouble later.

The research problems found throughout this book are designed to introduce you to research resources that may not have been covered in your first-year legal writing course and to reinforce your understanding that resolving employment law questions requires the ability to find and synthesize layers of federal and state law.[12] The problems are designed to supplement research skills that you have already obtained, not substitute for an advanced research course. To efficiently find resources to answer employment-law related questions, you should become familiar with:

1. The topical secondary sources available in your libraries or in online databases such as Westlaw, Lexis, and Bloomberg Law;

2. The information provided by the Equal Employment Opportunity Commission and the Department of Labor on their websites;[13]

3. The information provided by the departments of labor, fair employment practices agencies, and municipalities in the states in which you will practice; and

4. Public search engines to find specific laws and regulations.

---

[12] Although this book will not introduce local law, students should keep in mind that it could also significantly affect rights and obligations in the workplace. An attorney practicing in Chicago, for example, must consider Title VII, the Illinois Human Rights Act, and the Cook County and City of Chicago human rights laws. This layer of local law has become increasingly important as cities and localities supplant states as agents of change in labor and employment law by passing living-wage ordinances, protections for particular classifications, and paid family leave laws, to name just a few.

[13] EEOC, www.eeoc.gov (last visited July 7, 2019) and DEP'T OF LABOR, www.dol.gov (last visited July 7, 2019).

II. ESTABLISHING THE CLIENT RELATIONSHIP

You may have heard the lawyering truism that "a case is never as good as it is when it walks in the door." Although that is often true, the risk of being surprised by unfavorable facts or circumstances are minimized when attorneys know what questions to ask and what documents to seek. It also helps if you are a good judge of character and develop a healthy dose of skepticism.

To increase the likelihood of uncovering outcome-determinative facts, lawyers must be guided by two important questions: "What do I need to know?" and "Why do I need to know it?" Regardless of the substantive area in which you practice, governing law will always guide the answers to those questions.

Clients rarely walk into an attorney's office with a developed set of facts—a "story"—that neatly conforms to a cause of action or defense. It will be your job as an attorney to uncover the relevant facts through careful and detailed investigation of witnesses, documents, test results, site visits, and so on. Relevant facts are those that address an element of a claim or defense or provide important context; these are the outcome-determinative facts. Facts that establish a chronology and create the narrative background for the legally significant facts and answer the question "What story will you tell?" are also relevant. These facts are rarely uncovered in a single meeting with the client. Instead, attorneys regularly reevaluate what they know, and what they don't know, as facts emerge, and legal theories develop. Competent representation demands that lawyers establish "who, what, when, where, and how" and continually press clients to ensure their understanding of the facts remains current and accurate.

Many employment law textbooks start with the threshold question: "Who is an employee?" A parallel threshold question is: "Who or what is an employer?" The necessity of answering those questions at the outset will be repeatedly illuminated as you learn that certain individuals are denied the protections of employment laws, either because of their own status as "non-employees" or because their employers are beyond the reach of the law. Thus, ascertaining whether a legally cognizable "employer-employee" relationship exists provides necessary context for critically evaluating whether the law provides redress for the client's developing "story" and your developing mental checklist of questions should begin with establishing the nature of the employment relationship.

Exercise 1: Interviewing New Clients

Information for Jan Landry's Counsel

You work in a small law office representing individuals in a wide-range of labor and employment-law matters, including alleged discrimination, wage and hour violations, wrongful discharge, contract review, and unfair labor practices. One of your partners, who is preparing for a major trial, has asked you to interview a potential client. Conflicts checks have been performed and your firm may represent this individual, if you find a sufficient basis to do so. All you know is that her name is Jan Landry, she worked at Daisy Depot, and she believes she has been discriminated against.

To prepare for your interview, prepare a list of questions. Ask yourself "What do I need to know?" and "Why do I need to know it?"

Plaintiff's / Employee's Firm			
To *Associates representing Jan Landry*		**Date:** *9/22/YR-00*	**Time:** : AM / PM
From *Shari Allen*		**Phone:**	
Company / Address:		**Cell:**	
		Fax:	

Phone Memo

Message Text

A potential new client is coming in tomorrow to discuss bringing a wrongful termination action against her former employer. Shari had scheduled the meeting for 3:00 but can't make it and wants you to cover it.   Conference room 1250 is reserved for the meeting and the meeting is with Jan Landry. Shari apologizes if you have to reschedule previous plans. Please prepare notes to discuss with Shari when she returns. Conflicts check cleared.

Email: **Sign:** *Your Assistant*

| Phoned ☐ | Call back ☐ | Call returned ☐ | Wants to see you ☐ | Will call again ☐ | Was in ☐ | Urgent **X** |

Information for Daisy Depot's Counsel

You work in a medium-sized law firm that represents primarily corporate clients and municipalities. The labor and employment practice group, to which you are assigned, represents companies in a wide-range of employment-law matters, including compliance with workplace safety laws, alleged discrimination, wage and hour issues, wrongful discharge, and occasional constitutional claims. One of your partners, who is preparing for a major trial, has left you the following message to interview a current client of the firm—Daisy Depot—regarding a new employment-law matter. All you know is that the Vice President of Human Resources, Penelope Duquette, is concerned about the recent termination of a former Daisy Depot employee, Jan Landry.

To prepare for your interview, prepare a list of questions. Ask yourself "What do I need to know?" and "Why do I need to know it?"

Defense / Management Firm				
To: *Associates Representing Daisy Depot*			**Date:** *9/22/YR-00*	**Time:** : **AM / PM**
From: *Head of Practice Group – Harry Lead*			**Phone:**	
Company / Address:			**Cell:** **Fax:**	

Phone Memo

Message Text

Harry needs you to take his place on a scheduled video telephone call with Daisy Depot's VP of HR, Penelope Duquette, about a potential new matter regarding a former employee. The call is tomorrow at 3:00 but Harry can't attend. Conference room 4625 will be set up for the call. Harry will meet with you soon to review your notes. Duquette's phone number is 758-555-4321.

Email:					Sign: *Your Assistant*	
Phoned ☐	Call back ☐	Call returned ☐	Wants to see you ☐	Will call again ☐	Was in ☐	Urgent *X*

CHAPTER TWO

EMPLOYMENT DISCRIMINATION

I. AN OVERVIEW OF THE LAWYER'S ROLE

Notwithstanding the many federal, state, and local laws designed to shield workers from status-based discrimination and the length of time these laws have been in force, employers continue to discriminate in violation of the law.[1] Although hostility towards a protected class is not always the cause, stereotyping, scapegoating, and prejudice continue to infect the workplace. Even today, decisionmakers are not always as knowledgeable about employment law as they should be. Often, this is because their backgrounds do not include sufficient training in human resource management and employment law.

Most employment-law or employment-discrimination textbooks necessarily reserve the majority of their coverage of anti-discrimination law to the many federal laws prohibiting workplace discrimination. Most of those laws are enforced by the Equal Employment Opportunity Commission (EEOC), which has the authority to investigate claims of discrimination on the basis of race, color, religion, sex, national origin, age, disability, or genetic information. In 2018 alone, this agency received over 76,000 charges.[2]

Those charges do not include charges that were filed at state or local agencies based on individual characteristics that are not expressly protected by federal law, such as marital status or sexual orientation. Sometimes state laws are first to reflect changes in local demographics and the outcome of political debates. Because this often results in significant differences from state to state, it is simply not feasible to cover the diverse laws of fifty states in one course. However, employment lawyers who do not know and keep abreast of the text and interpretation of federal, state, and local anti-discrimination law, as well as the administrative process for enforcing those laws, put their clients' interests at risk and their own professional reputations and licenses in jeopardy.

It is arguably not enough for management-side employment lawyers to know what discriminatory practices are unlawful. Experienced attorneys attempt to understand the workplace dynamics that led to the discrimination in the first place. This enables them to address the cause of their clients' problems and steer their clients towards sound, nondiscriminatory employment decisions to reduce the likelihood of repeated violations.

Issues of employment discrimination comprise a significant percentage of an employment attorney's practice and, yet, it is not always possible to "know it when you see it." Although some decision-makers readily admit to discriminatory actions—especially when they result from paternalistic ideals rather than hostile attitudes towards a protected class—it is rare. In most cases, ferreting out discrimination requires the attorneys to engage in significant fact finding.

Through interviewing potential witnesses and decision-makers, reviewing and comparing personnel files, and reviewing corporate documents and employment handbooks, attorneys are looking for direct or circumstantial evidence of discrimination. Direct evidence can establish a material fact on its own, without the need for inferences, whereas circumstantial evidence tends to establish material facts by drawing inferences from more than one evidentiary source. A witness whose testimony is based on personal knowledge of what the witness saw, heard, or did may provide

---

[1] *See, e.g.,* Paula Span, *He Called Two Employees 'Dead Wood.' Two Sued for Age Discrimination*, N.Y. TIMES (July 6, 2018) (reporting on alleged age discrimination at Ohio State University).

[2] *Charge Statistics*, EEOC, https://www.eeoc.gov/eeoc/statistics/enforcement/charges.cfm (last visited July 6, 2019).

direct evidence. Subject to hearsay, authenticity, and other evidentiary rules governing admissibility, documents that articulate a course of action and underlying motives may also provide direct evidence. Of course, the credibility of witnesses and genuineness of documents must always be assessed.

When direct evidence is not available, attorneys must determine whether a combination of facts provide circumstantial evidence of discrimination. Different treatment for similarly situated employees, contradictory witness statements, changing or inconsistent reasons for an employment decision, and documents or testimony that cast doubt on an alleged motive for an employment decision may all be circumstantial evidence from which an inference of discrimination may be drawn.

Only after gathering facts from all available sources is an attorney able to preliminarily assess whether discrimination occurred. Whether particular discriminatory behavior is actionable depends on a variety of factors, however. Whether a company is an "employer" under relevant law, the size of the employer, whether it is public or private, and its industrial sector may all be relevant factors to that determination. Additional factors that might affect the viability of a worker's claim are the age of the worker, his or her terms of employment, and the nature of the job performed.

A finding that any one of those factors dooms a worker's claim under federal law is not the end of the analysis, however; it is only the beginning. The reach of state or local law may obviate the importance of factors that invalidated a claim under federal law. Moreover, state or local law might provide redress for claims that are not recognized under federal law. For attorneys representing the plaintiff, these distinctions will dictate the choice of forum to pursue a particular claim or require them to inform a sympathetic potential client that he or she does not have a cognizable claim under any of the relevant laws. For attorneys representing the defendant, these distinctions may suggest future counseling and training to avoid similar issues arising again.

Gathering facts, discerning motives, and applying the law to the facts must all be done at the inception of a case. Facts often change, and motives often become clearer as a case progresses, however. An attorney's obligation for fact-finding is never ending. The facts—and professional ethics—must guide an attorney's advice to and representation of their clients.

A. RESEARCHING EMPLOYMENT LAW

Although employers have a great deal of discretion in determining what education, skills, and backgrounds are necessary and desirable for their workforce, that discretion is limited by laws prohibiting discrimination, constraints on the information an employer may request, and education and licensing requirements for specific jobs. Because these factors are controlled by a combination of state and federal laws, even well-meaning employers can put themselves in jeopardy of discriminating if they do not know what laws apply in their jurisdictions. These can include city and county ordinances relating to employment practices, as well.

ARREST AND CONVICTION RECORDS

Considering the criminal-record information many law students have to provide on law-school and bar applications, you may be surprised that some jurisdictions limit an employer's right to request information about a job applicant's arrests or conviction records. The National Employment Law Project tracks the states, cities, and counties that are adopting "ban-the-box" or "fair-chance" policies that limit an employer's right to request such information.[3]

---

[3]   Beth Avery, *Ban the Box: U.S. Cities, Counties, and States Adopt Fair Hiring Policies*, NAT'L EMP'T LAW PROJECT (Apr. 19, 2019), https://www.nelp.org/publication/ban-the-box-fair-chance-hiring-state-and-local-guide/. For an analysis of ban-the-box laws, *see* Dallan Flake, *Do Ban-the-Box-Laws Really Work?*, 104 IOWA L. REV. 1079 (2019).

Similarly, many states protect individuals with arrest or conviction records through their anti-discrimination laws. When they exist, the scope of such protection varies considerably, ranging from prohibiting discrimination against employees and applicants based solely on expunged juvenile records[4] to more comprehensive protections.[5]

---

[4]   *E.g.,* West Virginia. *See* W. VA. CODE § 49–4–723 (Thomson Reuters, Westlaw through Reg. Sess. 2019).

[5]   *E.g.,* Massachusetts. *See* MASS. GEN. LAWS ch. 151B, § 4 (Thomson Reuters, Westlaw through Chapter 23 of 2019 1st Ann. Sess.).

Exercise 2: Arrest and Conviction Records

One of Daisy Depot's subsidiaries, ENCA, Co., is a factory that manufactures widgets for some of Daisy Depot's proprietary products. It employs forty-five employees. When an employee is on leave for an extended period, in cases of injury or illness, for example, it hires temporary workers to fill the vacancy. Although it must pay a premium to the temporary staffing firm that supplies the temporary workers, ENCA will sometimes hire one of the temporary workers for a regular job.

Until recently, Frankie worked at ENCA as a janitor. He was a temporary worker who was filling in for a janitor who was on leave because of a car accident. During the four months he worked for ENCA, the company found him to be pleasant and hard working. He had a good attitude and got along well with his supervisor and the other janitors.

When ENCA learned that its employee would not be able to return to the janitor job, it invited Frankie to apply for the job. In fact, because ENCA was so satisfied with his work, it offered Frankie the job contingent on the results of a routine background check. During the background check, however, ENCA learned that Frankie had a few arrests and convictions. He had been arrested for violating a local "open-container" law and for disorderly conduct. He was convicted of possessing a small amount of marijuana but not of intent to distribute. He was also convicted of DUI. All of these incidents happened between four and five years ago.

After learning about Frankie's background, ENCA told Frankie that it would not be able to hire him after all. A few weeks later, a lawyer informed ENCA that Frankie was planning to file a discrimination charge against ENCA because it had retracted the job offer. ENCA called you and the following conversation took place:

You: Why did you offer Frankie the job permanently?

ENCA: Because he was reliable and pleasant. He also took directions well and got along well with his supervisors and coworkers.

You: Why did you decide not to hire Frankie?

ENCA: Because of his arrest and conviction records.

You: Was there any other reason you did not hire Frankie?

ENCA: No. Frankie was great. We would have hired Frankie if it had not been for his arrest and conviction record.

You: Why was his record so important?

ENCA: We just don't think it's appropriate to have workers here who have criminal backgrounds of any kind.

ENCA wants your advice regarding how to defend against the discrimination charge if it is filed. Use any available research method to locate relevant anti-discrimination law, including accessing information provided at www.eeoc.gov and state agency websites. Your instructor will specify the state(s) you should consider in resolving this problem.

Please consider the following questions and identify the provisions of the laws, regulations, or guidance upon which your answers are based:

1)   What advice do you give ENCA based on your research of state law? Why?

2)   Would your advice be different if ENCA employed only twelve employees? Why?

3) Does federal law, regulation, or guidance address this question?

4) Does the specified state (or states) "ban the box" on employment applications?

5) What do you think the pros and cons are of prohibiting employers from evaluating arrest or conviction records when hiring or placing employees?

AGE DISCRIMINATION

According to the Bureau of Labor Statistics, the labor force participation rate for workers aged fifty-five and older—and in particular those aged sixty-five and older—has been increasing faster than the labor force participation of most other groups in the labor force.[6] This trend, which is driven by the number of aging "baby boomers" in the workforce, is likely to continue, with the labor force growth rate of workers aged seventy-five and older "expected to be about 86 percent, compared with a 5-percent increase for the labor force as a whole."[7] Despite these trends, the experience older workers bring to the workplace may not always be appreciated by their employers.[8]

Federal law has prohibited employment discrimination against applicants and employees age forty and older since 1967, when Congress passed the Age Discrimination in Employment Act of 1967 (ADEA). Many states have followed by including age discrimination in their anti-discrimination laws. In some cases, the state laws mirror federal law in terms of the age minimums of the workers protected and the size of the organizations subject to the law. In other cases, state laws reach more workers by reducing the minimum age of individuals protected or the size of organizations covered by the law. When faced with a potential age discrimination claim, lawyers must locate all applicable laws to determine whether the organization is an "employer" under federal or state law and whether the applicant or worker meets the minimum age threshold to be protected.

---

[6]   Mitra Toossi & Elka Torpey, *Older Workers: Labor force trends and career options*, BUREAU OF LABOR STATS. (May 2017), https://www.bls.gov/careeroutlook/2017/article/older-workers.htm; Mitra Toossi, *A Look at the Future of the U.S. Labor Force to 2060*, BUREAU OF LABOR STATS. (Sep. 2016), https://www.bls.gov/spotlight/2016/a-look-at-the-future-of-the-us-labor-force-to-2060/home.htm.

[7]   *See* Toossi & Torpey, *supra* note 6.

[8]   *See, e.g.*, JOSEPH COLEMAN, UNFINISHED WORK: THE STRUGGLE TO BUILD AN AGING AMERICAN WORKFORCE (2015).

Exercise 3: Age Discrimination

Sunflower Tech Solutions (STS), a small retail technology establishment with around a dozen employees, posted two management positions on its internal website, specifically seeking to promote current employees into these positions. After reviewing resumes and interviewing interested applicants, the 52-year-old office manager, Olivia Manning, narrowed the field to four. She personally knew all four candidates because they had worked for the company for some time. They all had relevant experience and college degrees, although their education and experience varied. Moreover, they were all generally well-spoken and professional. Able to hire only two, however, Ms. Manning eventually hired Anna and Bertha.

The two employees Ms. Manning promoted are close in age: Anna is 42-years-old and Bertha is 39-years-old. The two employees she rejected are not similar in age: Clara is 27-years-old and David is 60-years-old. Clara and David know the employees who were selected and believe themselves to be better qualified because of their sales performance.

During interviews, Ms. Manning stressed that appearance, competence, and credibility were vitally important for managers in the retail technology business. Based on some of Ms. Manning's questions and comments, Clara and David believe that Ms. Manning promoted Bertha and Anna because they fit her preconceived notion of the optimal age for the position.

Clara and David have come to you seeking advice on whether they should file charges against STS for discrimination. Your instructor will specify the state(s) you should consider in resolving this problem.

Please consider the following questions:

1) Are Clara and David protected from age discrimination under federal law?

2) Are Clara and David protected from age discrimination under state law?

3) Based on the text of the relevant law and the evidence you will need to prove discrimination, what further information do you need to more fully assess their claims and why?

4) What preliminary advice would you give Clara and David?

II. THE ADMINISTRATIVE PROCESS AT THE EEOC

A. INTRODUCTION TO THE ADMINISTRATIVE PROCESS AT THE EEOC

Representing or counseling clients regarding employment discrimination claims can constitute a significant percentage of an employment attorney's practice. To effectively represent those clients, it is therefore critical that employment lawyers be familiar with the administrative process and how it relates to subsequent court litigation.

With the Civil Rights Act of 1964, congress created the Equal Employment Opportunity Commission to enforce the employment provisions in Title VII of the Act, which forbids discrimination on the basis of race, color, religion, sex, and national origin. As additional laws were passed, the EEOC's enforcement responsibilities grew to include discrimination on the basis of unequal compensation under the Equal Pay Act (EPA), age under the Age Discrimination in Employment Act (ADEA), disability under the Americans with Disabilities Act (ADA), and genetic information under the Genetic Information Nondiscrimination Act (GINA). The EEOC also investigates charges of retaliation brought pursuant to those laws.

Over time, states created their own "fair employment practices agencies" ("FEPAs") with responsibility for enforcing state anti-discrimination laws. The laws enforced by these state agencies are similar to those enforced by EEOC. As previously mentioned, however, many state laws offer greater protection to workers than those provided by federal law. Because some discrimination claims only arise under state law, it is important to know state-law deadlines for filing discrimination charges, state-law standards for determining coverage, and state-law remedies for victims of discrimination.

Aggrieved individuals can file "charges" with either the EEOC or with the state FEPA. When an individual initially files the charge with a FEPA that has a work-sharing agreement with the EEOC, and the allegations raise claims under laws enforced by the EEOC, the FEPA will send a copy of the charge to the EEOC—or "dual file." The state FEPA will usually retain responsibility for processing the charge, however.

On the other hand, if the charge is initially filed with EEOC, and the charge is also covered by state or local law, the EEOC dual files the charge with the state or local FEPA but ordinarily retains the charge for processing, unless the state and federal charging requirements differ in a material way.[9] In recent years, the EEOC has moved much of the complaint process online, which makes it easier for individuals and employers to file, respond to, and track the status of discrimination charges. Some important changes in the transmittal of information between the parties have also accompanied this transition to the online process.

Where the charge is filed can affect what happens during and after the administrative process, including how the charge is investigated, what the limitations period is for bringing a charge, whether mediation is required, whether the parties must submit to a "fact-finding" hearing, and whether post-agency litigation occurs in state or federal court. Because state laws and investigative processes vary so widely, this book does not delve into the state administrative processes.

The number of discrimination charges filed at the EEOC has fluctuated over the years in response to new legislation and socio-economic factors. For example, age discrimination claims rose in conjunction with business reorganizations during the economic recession starting in 2008 and disability discrimination claims rose following the amendments to the ADA. In the aftermath of the

---

[9] Comprehensive information regarding EEOC procedures for employees and applicants, as well as employers and small business owners, can be found on the EEOC's website: https://www.eeoc.gov/.

recession, the years 2010 to 2012 saw a record high number of charges filed under all statutes. Since 2012, however, the total number has fallen.[10]

The EEOC publishes interesting and informative statistics that provide insight into the frequency and type of discrimination claims filed at the agency. For example, the data reveal that discharge- and harassment-related allegations are the most numerous claims made in charges brought under Title VII, the ADEA, ADA, EPA, and GINA.[11] It can be helpful for employment law attorneys to be aware of such trends—regardless of which side they represent.

SUMMARY OF THE EEOC PROCESS FOR PRIVATE EMPLOYERS[12]

Comprehensive information regarding EEOC procedures for employees/applicants and employers/small business owners can be found on the EEOC's website.[13] The following summary provides an overview of that information:

1. Complainant[14] files a charge of discrimination with the EEOC (or a FEPA).

    a. This can be accomplished online.

    b. The complainant need not be represented by counsel to file such a charge.[15]

    c. Charges must be filed at the EEOC generally within 180 or 300 days, depending on whether a state or local agency also prohibits the alleged discrimination.[16]

2. The EEOC will notify the respondent[17] of the charge within 10 days.

    a. The complainant and respondent have an opportunity to resolve the matter through mediation.[18]

3. The EEOC will investigate the charge to assess whether there is reasonable cause to believe that discrimination occurred.[19]

    a. Respondent will file a "position statement" and supporting documents in response to the charge within 30 days.

        i. Position statements and non-confidential documents will be shared with the complainant upon request.

        ii. The complainant has an opportunity to respond to the position statement within 20 days. The complainant's response will not be shared with the respondent.

        iii. The EEOC may request a site visit or witness interviews (but rarely does).

        iv. The respondent should be represented by counsel.

---

[10] For charge statistics filed at the EEOC over the years, *see Charge Statistics, supra* note 2. These do not include charged filed at state or local FEPAs.

[11] *See Statutes by Issue*, EEOC, https://www.eeoc.gov/eeoc/statistics/enforcement/statutes_by_issue.cfm (last visited July 7, 2019) and *Bases by Issue*, EEOC, https://www.eeoc.gov/eeoc/statistics/enforcement/bases_by_issue.cfm (last visited July 7, 2019).

[12] Federal employees and job applicants have similar protections, but different charge processes. *See, e.g., How to File a Charge of Employment Discrimination*, EEOC, https://www.eeoc.gov/employees/howtofile.cfm (last visited July 7, 2019); *What You Can Expect After You File a Charge*, EEOC, https://www.eeoc.gov/employees/process.cfm (last visited July 7, 2019); and *What You Can Expect After a Charge is Filed*, EEOC, https://www.eeoc.gov/employers/process.cfm (last visited July 7, 2019).

[13] EEOC, https://www.eeoc.gov (last visited July 7, 2019).

[14] The individual bringing the charge is called either the "charging party" or the "complainant" during the administrative process. For brevity's sake, the term "complainant" will be used.

[15] *How to File a Charge of Employment Discrimination, supra* note 12.

[16] *Time Limits for Filing a Charge*, EEOC, https://www.eeoc.gov/employees/timeliness.cfm (last visited July 7, 2019).

[17] The company responding to the charge is called the "respondent" during the administrative process.

[18] *Mediation*, EEOC, https://www.eeoc.gov/eeoc/mediation/index.cfm (last visited July 7, 2019).

[19] *What You Can Expect After a Charge is Filed, supra* note 12.

4. The complainant and respondent have an opportunity to settle the claims.

5. If the EEOC is unable to find reasonable cause to believe that discrimination occurred, it will issue a Dismissal and Notice of Rights to the complainant, informing the complainant that he or she has 90 days to file suit in federal court. Respondent will also receive a copy of this Notice.

6. If the EEOC finds reasonable cause, it will attempt to resolve the matter through its conciliation process.

7. If conciliation fails, the EEOC may file suit against respondent or issue a Right to Sue to the complainant.

B. THE CHARGE OF DISCRIMINATION

Except for wage discrimination claims brought under the Equal Pay Act (EPA) or race discrimination claims under § 1981, plaintiffs must exhaust their administrative remedies before filing a discrimination lawsuit in federal court by filing a charge[20] within the mandatory time limit with the EEOC.[21] Charges filed with the EEOC must put the agency and respondent on notice regarding the nature and basis of the discrimination alleged. In other words, it is insufficient to simply allege discrimination; rather the complainant must identify the harm suffered and how that harm was related to the complainant's protected class. Requiring administrative exhaustion affords an opportunity for the EEOC and the parties to settle disputes and avoid further litigation. This requirement also puts employers on notice regarding the claims likely to be filed against them.

Because complainants are often unrepresented during the administrative process, allegations contained in the charge are sometimes minimal and unclear. The sufficiency of the charge is not an onerous standard, however: "[e]ven if a charge fails to contain the specified information, it may still be sufficient, provided it is 'a written statement sufficiently precise to identify the parties, and to describe generally the action or practices complained of.' "[22] Even though the standards are minimal, the allegations in the charge most often articulate a *prima facie* case of discrimination by stating facts purporting to show direct evidence of discrimination or indirect evidence sufficient to raise an inference of discrimination.

It behooves the complainant to be as thorough as possible, even though the respondent must respond to the charge regardless of how artfully it captures the alleged basis for the charge. While the standards are not exacting, incomplete or incoherent charges may limit a plaintiff's later options. Because subsequent federal court actions are limited to the "scope of the charge," complainants may be barred from raising claims that were not readily identifiable from the allegations made in the initial EEOC charge. As the example mediation opening statement on pages 34–35 shows, complainants often cover their bases by alleging multiple grounds of discrimination.

---

[20] Individuals begin the process by completing an intake questionnaire providing information to support their claim of discrimination. The EEOC is often responsible for drafting the charge based on the intake form.

[21] Statutory time limitations are summarized by the EEOC at *Time Limits for Filing a Charge*, EEOC, https://www.eeoc.gov/employees/timeliness.cfm (last visited July 7, 2019). *See also* 42 U.S.C. § 2000e–5 (2012).

[22] Jones v. UPS, Inc., 502 F.3d 1176, 1184 (10th Cir. 2007) (quoting 29 C.F.R. § 1601.12(b) (2012)).

Exercise 4:   The Relationship Between the Charge and the Complaint

Review the charge and complaint on the following pages.

Please consider the following questions regarding the EEOC charge filed by the plaintiff Natia Barrow:

1) Identify on what basis Barrow claims that she was discriminated against.

2) If it is clear from the face of the charge, identify the discrimination theory and analytical paradigm under which Barrow is proceeding.

3) Does the charge contain all of the necessary information?

4) Is the charge procedurally deficient in any way?

Please consider the following questions regarding the complaint filed by Barrow in federal court:

1) Does Barrow's complaint raise the same issues she raised in her charge?

2) If you were CableCom's counsel, how would you respond procedurally to Barrow's complaint and why? Would you file an answer or a motion?

3) If you were Barrow's counsel, what revisions, if any, would you have suggested she make to the charge before finalizing it and why?

4) Does Count I (section III) state a claim upon which relief can be granted? Why or why not?

5) Does Count II (section IV) state a claim upon which relief can be granted? Why or why not?

6) In light of all facts alleged, are any deficiencies curable by filing an amended complaint? Why or why not?

Charge of Discrimination

CHARGE OF DISCRIMINATION This form is affected by the Privacy Act of 1974. See enclosed Privacy Act Statement and other information before completing this form.	Charge Presented To: ☐ FEPA ☒ EEOC	Agency(ies) Charge No(s): **172-2006-00085**

EmLand Human Relations Commission		and EEOC
State or local Agency, if any		

Name *(indicate Mr., Ms., Mrs.)* **Ms. Natia Barrow**	Home Phone *(Incl. Area Code)* **(555) 558-5557**	Date of Birth **07-21-1956**
Street Address **167 Jackson Lane**	City, State and ZIP Code **Greenville, EmLand 12345**	

Named is the Employer, Labor Organization, Employment Agency, Apprenticeship Committee, or State or Local Government Agency That I Believe Discriminated Against Me or Others. *(If more than two, list under PARTICULARS below.)*

Name **CableCom**	No. Employees, Members **101-200**	Phone No. *(Include Area Code)*
Street Address **1717 Ark Street**	City, State and ZIP Code **Greenville, EmLand 12345**	

Name	No. Employees, Members	Phone No. *(Include Area Code)*
Street Address	City, State and ZIP Code	

DISCRIMINATION BASED ON *(Check appropriate box(es).)*	DATE(S) DISCRIMINATION TOOK PLACE
☐ RACE ☐ COLOR ☒ SEX ☐ RELIGION ☐ NATIONAL ORIGIN ☐ RETALIATION ☐ AGE ☐ DISABILITY ☐ GENETIC INFORMATION ☐ OTHER *(Specify)*	Earliest Latest **12-21-2004** **12-21-2004** ☐ CONTINUING ACTION

THE PARTICULARS ARE *(If additional paper is needed, attach extra sheet(s))*:

1. I started my employment with CableCom on November 30, 1986. I held the position of Splicing Technician. On December 31, 2004, I was discharged from my position.

2. On December 21, 2004, I had a meeting with Al Nemet, Jr., Local Manager, and Bob Weidner, Second Level Manager. They told me that I was discharged for falsification of time sheets, violation of work rules, and unauthorized use of Company vehicle.

3. I believe that the respondent discriminated against me because of my sex, female, in violation of Title VU of the Civil Rights Act of 1964, as amended, in that males were not discharged as I was, even though they engaged in infractions of comparable seriousness.

I want this charge filed with both the EEOC and the State or local Agency, if any. I will advise the agencies if I change my address or phone number and I will cooperate fully with them in the processing of my charge in accordance with their procedures.	NOTARY -- *When necessary for State and Local Agency* *Requirements* *N. Tary*
I declare under penalty of perjury that the above is true and correct. *1-15-2005* *Natia Barrow* Date Charging Party Signature	I swear or affirm that I have read the above charge and that it is true to the best of my knowledge, information and belief. SIGNATURE OF COMPLAINANT SUBSCRIBED AND SWORN TO BEFORE ME THIS DATE

Complaint

IN THE UNITED STATES DISTRICT COURT FOR THE WESTERN DISTRICT OF EMLAND

NATIA BARROW,	)	
	)	
Plaintiff	)	
	)	Civil Action
No: CABLECOM, INC., and	)	
ALLEN M. NEMET,	)	
	)	
Defendants	)	

COMPLAINT

Plaintiff, Natia Barrow, by and through her counsel, Susan N. Gould, Esq., for her complaint against CableCom, Inc., respectfully alleges and states as follows:

I.   Parties and Jurisdiction

1.   Plaintiff is an adult individual who resides at 167 Jackson Lane, Greenville, EmLand 12345.

2.   Defendant CableCom, Inc., is a corporation organized under the laws of the EmLand with its principle business address at1717 Ark Street, Greenville, EmLand, 13456.

3.   Defendant Allen Nemet is an adult individual who at all material times was an employee of Defendant CableCom, Inc.

4.   This Court has jurisdiction pursuant to 28 U.S.C. § 1331.

5.   This action is authorized and instituted pursuant to Title VII of the Civil Rights Act of 1964, as amended.

6.   Venue is proper in this Court pursuant to 28 U.S.C. § 1391 because all pertinent acts took place in the Western District of EmLand.

7.   Within 180 days after the alleged unlawful employment practice complained of herein, the Plaintiff filed a charge of discrimination with the Equal Employment Opportunity Commission, satisfying the requirements of 42 U.S.C. § 2000e–5, and on March 30, 2006, less than 90 days prior to the filing of this Complaint, the Commission issued to Plaintiff a Notice of Right to Sue with respect to Plaintiff's charges.

II.   Factual Background

8.   Plaintiff commenced employment with the Defendant on November 30, 1986.

9.   At all material times, Plaintiff was employed as a Splicing Technician at the West Chester Work Center.

10.   At all material times, Defendant Nemet was Plaintiff's immediate supervisor.

11.   On December 21, 2004, Plaintiff attended a meeting with her immediate supervisor, Al Nemet, and Bob Weidner, Second Level Manager.

12. At that meeting, Plaintiff was advised that she was discharged from employment, based upon the following allegations:

   1. Falsification of overtime on time sheets for November 22, 23, and 24, 2004;

   2. Talking on the phone from approximately 7:00 a.m. to 12:00 noon at the West Chester Work Center on December 7, 2004; and,

   3. Unauthorized use of a work vehicle on December 18, 2004.

13. Plaintiff did not falsify overtime sheets on November 22, 23, and 24, 2004, or at any other time during her employment with the Defendant.

14. Plaintiff did not talk on the phone from approximately 7:00 a.m. to 12:00 noon on December 7, 2004, in violation of work rules.

15. Plaintiff's use of a company vehicle on December 18, 2004 was not unauthorized.

III. Disparate Treatment

16. Male employees of the Defendant have engaged in alleged infractions of comparable seriousness and were not discharged.

17. Defendant has discriminated against Plaintiff because of her sex, female, in violation of Title VII of the Civil Rights Act, as amended.

IV. Hostile Work Environment

18. Defendant Allen Nemet acted to create and maintain a hostile work environment for the Plaintiff because of her gender, by engaging in the following:

   a. Addressing Plaintiff in a demeaning and condescending manner;

   b. Employing terms inappropriate for a workplace in addressing Plaintiff, such as "kiddo," and "babe";

   c. Altering Plaintiff's time sheets without her knowledge or consent;

   d. Deliberately depriving Plaintiff of work hours made available to other crew members; and,

   e. Fabricating and pursuing the baseless allegations against the Plaintiff which led to her dismissal.

19. Defendant Nemet's actions have created a hostile work environment as defined by the courts construing Title VII.

20. At all material times, the actions of Defendant Nemet were undertaken with the knowledge of his supervisors at Defendant CableCom, Inc.

21. The effect of the policies and practices pursued by Defendant Nemet and with the knowledge Defendant CableCom, Inc., discriminated against the Plaintiff in such a way as to jeopardize Plaintiff's job, deprive her of her employment opportunities, and otherwise adversely affect her status as an employee because of her gender.

V. Jury Demand

22. Plaintiff hereby demands a trial by jury of all issues triable by a jury.

WHEREFORE, Plaintiff respectfully requests that this Court award for the Plaintiff and against the Defendant the following:

   a. Reinstatement to her position of Splicing Technician;

b.   Back pay from the date of her termination plus appropriate pension adjustments;

c.   Reasonable attorney's fees; and,

d.   Such other relief as may be appropriate and just.

Respectfully submitted:

/s/ Susan N. Gould
Susan N. Gould, Esquire
EM ID# 40077
111 North Main Street
Suite 106
Greenville, EmLand 12345

Exercise 5: Identifying Claims

Information for Jan Landry's Counsel

MEMORANDUM

TO: Shari Allen—Supervising Attorney

FROM: Attorneys representing Jan Landry

DATE: September 25, YR-00

RE: Meeting with Jan Landry on September 23, YR-00

Thank you for giving me the opportunity to meet with Jan Landry on September 23. We had an interesting discussion about her dispute with her former employer, Daisy Depot. At your request, I have summarized our meeting in the attached confidential memorandum. Please let me know if there is anything further that I can do to assist on this matter.

[CONFIDENTIAL INFORMATION FOR JAN LANDRY'S COUNSEL
TO BE PROVIDED BY INSTRUCTOR]

MEMORANDUM & ASSIGNMENT

TO: New Associate

FROM: Shari Allen

DATE: October 1, YR-00

RE: Jan Landry

I have reviewed your notes and Ms. Landry appears to have colorable claims of discrimination against Daisy Depot. After reviewing the EEOC Charge form, please prepare a draft of the Charge including all of the potential claims she can assert. If there is any information missing, please request it from her.

[BLANK EEOC FORM 5 PROVIDED SEPARATELY]

Information for Daisy Depot's Counsel

MEMORANDUM

TO: Harry Lead—Head of Labor and Employment Law Practice Group

FROM: Associates representing Daisy Depot

DATE: September 25, YR-00

RE: Daisy Depot/Jan Landry Matter

Harry, I met with Daisy Depot's VP of H.R., Penelope Duquette, via video about the situation in its Woodstock store, which is one of its bigger stores. Since Bob is the paralegal assigned to Daisy Depot, I took the liberty of asking him to join the meeting to make sure that we would have comprehensive notes.

Apparently, one of the regional managers, David Walker, was updating Ms. Duquette on recent personnel problems he has been experiencing. Ms. Duquette is particularly concerned about what Walker told her about the reasons he fired a long-time employee, Jan Landry. Although we would need to verify the facts, a confidential synopsis of the information she told me follows. Please let me know what else you need. Thanks.

[CONFIDENTIAL INFORMATION FOR DAISY DEPOT'S COUNSEL
TO BE PROVIDED BY INSTRUCTOR]

MEMORANDUM & ASSIGNMENT

TO: Junior Associate

FROM: Harry Lead

DATE: October 1, YR-00

RE: Daisy Depot/Jan Landry Matter

I have reviewed your notes and would like to anticipate any colorable discrimination claims Ms. Landry appears to have against Daisy Depot. To assist you, I have attached an EEOC Charge form to this memo. After reviewing the form, please draft a letter to Ms. Duquette regarding all of the potential claims Ms. Landry can assert. For your information, a blank discrimination charge form follows. Ms. Duquette's address is:

Daisy Depot

2214 Hoffmann Estates Rd.

Chico, EmLand 44441

If there are other compliance issues you believe Daisy Depot should address, please include those.

Charge of Discrimination

CHARGE OF DISCRIMINATION This form is affected by the Privacy Act of 1974. See enclosed Privacy Act Statement and other information before completing this form.	Charge Presented To: ☐ FEPA ☐ EEOC	Agency(ies) Charge No(s):
		and EEOC

State or local Agency, if any

Name (indicate Mr., Ms., Mrs.)	Home Phone (Incl. Area Code)	Date of Birth
Street Address	City, State and ZIP Code	

Named is the Employer, Labor Organization, Employment Agency, Apprenticeship Committee, or State or Local Government Agency That I Believe Discriminated Against Me or Others. (_If more than two, list under PARTICULARS below._)

Name	No. Employees, Members	Phone No. (Include Area Code)
Street Address	City, State and ZIP Code	
Name	No. Employees, Members	Phone No. (Include Area Code)
Street Address	City, State and ZIP Code	

DISCRIMINATION BASED ON (Check appropriate box(es).)	DATE(S) DISCRIMINATION TOOK PLACE
☐ RACE ☐ COLOR ☐ SEX ☐ RELIGION	Earliest Latest
☐ NATIONAL ORIGIN ☐ RETALIATION ☐ AGE ☐ DISABILITY	
☐ GENETIC INFORMATION ☐ OTHER (Specify)	☐ CONTINUING ACTION

THE PARTICULARS ARE (If additional paper is needed, attach extra sheet(s)):

I want this charge filed with both the EEOC and the State or local Agency, if any. I will advise the agencies if I change my address or phone number and I will cooperate fully with them in the processing of my charge in accordance with their procedures.	NOTARY – _When necessary for State and Local Agency Requirements_
I declare under penalty of perjury that the above is true and correct.	I swear or affirm that I have read the above charge and that it is true to the best of my knowledge, information and belief. SIGNATURE OF COMPLAINANT SUBSCRIBED AND SWORN TO BEFORE ME THIS DATE
_____ Date Charging Party Signature	

C. MEDIATION

After a charge is filed with the EEOC, the parties may be asked or required to participate in mediation to resolve the matter.[23] A resolution in mediation does not lead to a finding on the issues raised in the charge; the goal of mediation is to settle a case with the assistance of a neutral party, regardless of the merits of the case. Although the parties can negotiate a settlement with the assistance of counsel at any time, an early mediated settlement can benefit both parties.

The EEOC identifies the following incentives for the parties to participate in mediation.

1. **"Mediation is free.**

   EEOC's National Mediation Program is available at no cost to the parties.

2. **Mediation is fair and neutral.**

   Parties have an equal say in the process and they, not the mediator, decide the terms of the settlement. There is no determination of guilt or innocence in the process.

3. **Mediation saves time and money.**

   Mediation usually occurs early in the charge process, and many mediations are completed in one meeting. Legal or other representation is optional but not required.

4. **Mediation is confidential.**

   All parties sign a confidentiality agreement. Information disclosed during mediation will not be revealed to anyone, including EEOC investigative or legal staff.

5. **Mediation avoids litigation.**

   Mediation costs less than a lawsuit and avoids the uncertainty of a judicial outcome.

6. **Mediation fosters cooperation.**

   Mediation fosters a problem-solving approach to complaints and workplace disruptions are reduced. With an investigation, even if the charge is dismissed by EEOC, underlying problems may remain, affecting others in the workforce.

7. **Mediation improves communication.**

   Mediation provides a neutral and confidential setting in which the parties can openly discuss their views on the underlying dispute. Enhanced communication can lead to mutually satisfactory resolutions.

8. **Mediation helps to discover the real issues in your workplace.**

   Parties share information, which can lead to a better understanding of issues affecting the workplace.

9. **Mediation allows you to design your own solution.**

   A neutral third party assists the parties in reaching a voluntary, mutually beneficial resolution. Mediation can resolve all issues important to the parties, not just the underlying legal dispute.

10. **With mediation, everyone wins.**

    An independent survey showed 96% of all respondents and 91% of all charging parties who used mediation would use it again."[24]

---

[23] For more comprehensive information, *see Mediation, supra* note 18.

[24] *10 Reasons to Mediate*, EEOC, https://www.eeoc.gov/eeoc/mediation/10reasons.cfm (last visited July 7, 2019).

For the complainant, there are few reasons not to participate in the mediation process—it is a free and relatively quick way of altering the status quo, even if the complainant does not get the full relief to which he or she feels entitled. As long as the respondent is willing to offer the complainant some relief, mediation can also benefit the respondent by expeditiously resolving the matter without incurring significant attorney's fees.

The most common reason that respondents are reluctant to participate in mediation is their perception of the charge as lacking merit.[25] Employers may fear that settling an unmeritorious charge will encourage other unhappy employees or applicants to file their own charges. Depending on the workplace, and the nature of the charge, this can be a legitimate concern.

Whether you advise your client to mediate will depend on your assessment of the likelihood of an unfavorable finding at the termination of the administrative process; potential damages; the burdens and costs of proceeding, including the emotional and disruptive effects on your client and her opponent; the likelihood of future litigation; and the possibility of disclosing unfavorable information to the other side early in the process. Attorneys should undertake a comprehensive risk-benefit analysis based on their previous experience and their understanding of each party's strengths and weaknesses.

Although the EEOC posits that "with mediation, everyone wins,"[26] settling any case requires compromise and, thus, everyone also "loses." Therefore, preparing for mediation requires identifying a range of acceptable settlement options for your client and anticipating what the other side is willing to accept. Additionally, settling a charge through mediation does not necessarily require a monetary settlement. By keeping an open mind and listening to the complainant's grievance, a respondent may be able to devise a creative satisfactory solution.

In many cases, the role of an attorney at the mediation itself is limited to providing advice and counsel to the client. In such cases, the mediator may ask the attorneys not to speak for the client and to let the mediator control the proceedings. Although this may be the case, many attorneys prepare a persuasive opening statement to set the stage or, at the least, outline the perceived strengths of their clients' positions. As the following example demonstrates, an outline can also serve to keep the parties focused on the material allegations the complainant asserts.

Most of the same principles regarding the professional and ethical considerations that arise during settlement negotiations are equally important during mediation. Therefore, the information discussed in Part D, Settling Claims, on page 46, is also relevant here. Even if mediation fails, the process can provide insight into the merits of the charge and of the parties' relative strengths and weaknesses. The information learned during mediation can be used in the future if the parties try to negotiate a settlement on their own.

---

[25] *See generally* E. Patrick McDermott et al., *An Investigation of the Reasons for the Lack of Employer Participation in the EEOC Mediation Program* (Dec. 10, 2003), https://www.eeoc.gov/eeoc/mediation/report/study3/index.html.

[26] *10 Reasons to Mediate, supra* note 24.

Example of Mediation Opening Statement

Apple v. American Lung Foundation
Mediation & Settlement Talks

I. **AMERICAN LUNG FOUNDATION (ALF)**

   1. Created in 1976, it is the only voluntary organization in the nation providing a voice for 30 million Americans with lung disease.

   2. ALF provides financial support for medical research, education for medical professionals, and advocacy and information for patients and their families.

II. **ALF St. Larry/Tina City Office**

   3. Locally, ALF operates from its St. Larry office. Ms. Bauble is the Executive Director of that office supervising a Community Events Coordinator and a Program Manager

III. **Ms. Apple**

   4. Ms. Apple was hired as a Community Events Coordinator (CEC) for the Tina City area.

   5. As a CEC, Ms. Apple spent about 90% of her time raising funds for ALF and about 10% of her time doing programming activities.

   6. Ms. Apple was to work from her home and was to be the sole ALF representative in Tina City.

IV. **Discharge**

   7. Ms. Apple was discharged in November 2008 because of her fundraising performance.

   8. Ms. Apple was not alone. With the economy beginning its tailspin, ALF needed to cut costs. In the months of October, November, and December, ALF discharged 5 other employees from across the entire organization in an effort to cut costs. It also cancelled contributions to its 401(k) plan and froze salaries across the board.

V. **No Legal Basis for Claims**

   9. Age Claim

      a. Ms. Apple's discharge was part of an effort to reduce staff to save money and was not related to her age.

      b. Between October and December, ALF terminated five other under-performing employees ranging in age from 25-years-old to 43-years-old.

      c. Further, Ms. Bauble was the one who hired Ms. Apple, and, in such cases, there is a strong inference against finding that Ms. Bauble would have discriminated against Ms. Apple based on her age.

      d. Ms. Bauble was not even the one who ultimately made the decision to discharge Ms. Apple. That decision was made by Becky French, ALF's Chief Development Officer who did not know Ms. Apple's age until she filed her charge with the EEOC.

10. Disability Claim

    a.   Ms. Apple may not even be "disabled" as defined by the ADA. Her charge does not identify any disability.

    b.   She never informed ALF that she was disabled.

    c.   She never requested any accommodations from ALF for any disability.

11. Retaliation Claim

    a.   While Ms. Apple may have complained to others at ALF about Ms. Bauble's supervision of her, she never even hinted that she thought that Ms. Bauble was treating her differently because of her age or disability.

    b.   There is simply no evidence that Ms. Apple engaged in any protected activity necessary to support a retaliation claim.

12. Wrongful Discharge Claim

    a.   For the same reasons, any state claim is also faulty.

    b.   Even if a claim is available, Ms. Apple's age, disability, and complaints were not the reason for her discharge—let alone the exclusive reason as required under EmLand law.

13. Wage & Hour Claim

    a.   Ms. Apple was properly classified as exempt from the overtime requirements of the Fair Labor Standards Act.

    b.   She was the sole ALF representative in the Tina City office, she raised funds, represented ALF at events, scheduled and planned major fundraisers—all with little or no direct supervision.

    c.   Department of Labor (DOL) has found that similar employees are exempt under the Administrative exemption.

VI. Conclusion

14. In sum, Ms. Apple was discharged as an under-performing fundraiser when ALF needed to cut costs in response to a downturn in the economy. That decision was wholly unrelated to her age, purported disability, or any complaints she may have made.

Exercise 6:   Preparing for Mediation

Information for Jan Landry's Counsel

MEMORANDUM

TO: Attorneys representing Jan Landry

FROM: Shari Allen—Supervising Attorney

DATE: October 24, YR-00

RE: Meeting with Jan Landry on September 23, YR-00

Thank you for helping Jan with her EEOC discrimination charge. The EEOC has sent us a copy of the charge, as well as information regarding its mediation program. These documents follow on pages 41–44. I talked it over with Jan, and she does want to try to resolve the charge and move on in one way or another. To assist us in preparing for the mediation, please provide:

1)   A one-to-two paragraph summary of your analysis of the strengths and weakness of Jan's position,

2)   Suggestions regarding what Jan should or could consider accepting in order to settle the case, and

3)   A brief outline of your opening statement.

October 20, YR-00

Jan Landry
3 Paper Tiger Way
Tina City, EmLand 67401

Re: Charge No. 191919 / Landry & Daisy Depot

Dear Ms. Landry,

Enclosed please find a copy of the charge you filed against Daisy Depot. We have sent this charge to the company's Vice President of Human Resources, Penelope Duquette. To encourage expeditious resolution of your charge, I invite you to participate in voluntary confidential mediation with Daisy Depot. You can explore the benefits of mediation on our website at: https://www.eeoc.gov/eeoc/mediation/10reasons.cfm. For your information, I enclose a sample of a confidentiality agreement, which we will complete if Daisy Depot agrees to the mediation, and a copy of our form settlement agreement, which we will complete if you and Daisy Depot reach a satisfactory resolution of the charge.

If you would like to discuss this further, please contact me. I will let you know if Daisy Depot is amenable to mediation. If the matter is not settled through mediation, the EEOC will investigate the charge.

Regards,

Lindsey A. Kristy
Lindsey A. Kristy
Equal Employment Opportunity Commission

Information for Daisy Depot's Counsel

MEMORANDUM

TO: Associates representing Daisy Depot

FROM: Harry Lead—Head of Labor and Employment Law Practice Group

DATE: October 24, YR-00

RE: Daisy Depot/Jan Landry Matter

Jan Landry did file a charge of discrimination against Daisy Depot. The EEOC has sent us a copy of the charge as well as information regarding its mediation program. These documents follow on pages 41–44. I have discussed mediation with Daisy Depot and the company wishes to participate. To assist us in preparing for the mediation, please provide:

1) A one-to-two paragraph summary of your analysis of the strengths and weakness of Daisy Depot's position,

2) Suggestions regarding what the company should or could consider offering to settle the case, and

3) A brief outline of your opening statement.

October 20, YR-00

Penelope Duquette
Vice President of Human Resources
2214 Hoffmann Estates Rd.
Chico, EmLand 44441

Re: Charge No. 191919 / Landry & Daisy Depot

Dear Ms. Duquette,

Enclosed please find a copy of the discrimination charge Ms. Jan Landry has filed against Daisy Depot. To encourage expeditious resolution of this charge, I invite you to participate in voluntary confidential mediation with Ms. Landry. You can explore the benefits of mediation on our website at: https://www.eeoc.gov/eeoc/mediation/10reasons.cfm. For your information, I enclose a sample of a confidentiality agreement, which we will complete if you and Ms. Landry agree to the mediation, and a copy of our form settlement agreement, which we will complete if the mediation results in a satisfactory resolution of the charge.

If you would like to discuss this further, please contact me. Should you or Ms. Landry decline mediation or if the matter is not settled through mediation, the EEOC will investigate the charge and Daisy Depot will be required to submit a position statement and other information.

Regards,

Lindsey A. Kristy
Lindsey A. Kristy
Equal Employment Opportunity Commission

1410 Generous Road, Suite 60, Tina City, Emland 55552
(785) 555-1345

Charge of Discrimination

CHARGE OF DISCRIMINATION This form is affected by the Privacy Act of 1974. See enclosed Privacy Act Statement and other information before completing this form.	Charge Presented To: X FEPA X EEOC	Agency(ies) Charge No(s): **77777** **191919**
		and EEOC

State or local Agency, if any

Name (indicate Mr., Ms., Mrs.) **Ms. Jan Landry**	Home Phone (Incl. Area Code) **(785) 555-1234**	Date of Birth **YR-39**
Street Address **3 Paper Tiger Way**	City, State and ZIP Code **Woodstock, EmLand 67401**	

Named is the Employer, Labor Organization, Employment Agency, Apprenticeship Committee, or State or Local Government Agency That I Believe Discriminated Against Me or Others. (*If more than two, list under PARTICULARS below.*)

Name **Daisy Depot**	No. Employees, Members **130**	Phone No. (Include Area Code) **789-666-1234**
Street Address **1717 W. 32nd St.**	City, State and ZIP Code **Woodstock, EmLand 67402**	
Name	No. Employees, Members	Phone No. (Include Area Code)
Street Address	City, State and ZIP Code	

DISCRIMINATION BASED ON (Check appropriate box(es).)	DATE(S) DISCRIMINATION TOOK PLACE
X RACE [ ] COLOR X SEX X RELIGION X NATIONAL ORIGIN X RETALIATION X AGE [ ] DISABILITY [ ] GENETIC INFORMATION X OTHER (Specify) **Harassment**	Earliest: **05/YR-01** Latest: **09/01/YR-00** [ ] CONTINUING ACTION

THE PARTICULARS ARE (If additional paper is needed, attach extra sheet(s)):

1. I am an Asian-American female.
2. I have been employed at Daisy Depot since 2003. I have always performed well, and, in fact, I was promoted to store manager.
3. In YR-02, Mr. David Walker became the regional manager. That is when my problems started.
4. On May 10, YR-01 and February YR-00, Walker told me to fire two different employees because they refused to work on Sunday due to religious reasons. I told him that I couldn't because that would be religious discrimination. Mr. Walker cursed at me and said I should "man up" or he would suspend me for failing to follow orders and for "complaining to him about this stuff."
5. Because I refused to violate the law, I was reprimanded and suspended without pay for two days.
6. Mr. Walker was always referring to the Woodstock store as the "Lady's Store" and always making sexist comments like that. It was hostile and embarrassing.

On September 1, YR-00, Mr. Walker fired me. He claimed that the reason was because of low sales numbers for my store. I was replaced by a white male. Because I always had good sales numbers, I believe the real reason was because I am an Asian woman who refused to discriminate against employees because of their religious beliefs.

I want this charge filed with both the EEOC and the State or local Agency, if any. I will advise the agencies if I change my address or phone number and I will cooperate fully with them in the processing of my charge in accordance with their procedures.	NOTARY – When necessary for State and Local Agency Requirements
I declare under penalty of perjury that the above is true and correct.	I swear or affirm that I have read the above charge and that it is true to the best of my knowledge, information and belief. SIGNATURE OF COMPLAINANT
Oct YR-00 *Jan Landry* Date Charging Party Signature	*Jan Landry* SUBSCRIBED AND SWORN TO BEFORE ME THIS DATE

Confidentiality Agreement

CHARGE NUMBER:

1.   The parties agree to participate voluntarily in mediation in an effort to resolve the charge(s) filed with the EEOC.

2.   The parties agree that all matters discussed during the mediation are confidential, unless otherwise discoverable, and cannot be used as evidence in any subsequent administrative or judicial proceeding. Confidentiality, however, will not extend to threats of imminent physical harm or incidents of actual violence that occur during the mediation.

3.   Any communications between the ADR Coordinator and the mediator(s) and/or the parties are considered dispute resolution communications with a neutral party and will be kept confidential.

4.   The parties agree not to subpoena the mediator(s) or compel the mediator(s) to produce any documents provided by a party in any pending or future administrative or judicial proceeding. The mediator(s) will not voluntarily testify on behalf of a party in any pending or future administrative or judicial proceeding. The parties further agree that the mediator(s) will be held harmless for any claim arising from the mediation process.

5.   Mediation sessions will not be tape-recorded or transcribed by the EEOC, the mediator, or any of the participants. All information, including all notes, records, or documents generated during the course of the mediation, shall be destroyed at the conclusion of the session. Parties or their representatives are not prohibited from retaining their own notes. However, EEOC will not maintain any such notes or records as part of its record-keeping procedures.

6.   If a settlement is reached by all the parties, the agreement shall be reduced to writing and, when signed, shall be binding upon all parties to the agreement. If the charge(s) is not resolved through mediation, it is understood by the parties that the charge(s) will be transferred to the investigative unit for further processing.

_____   _____
Charging Party   Date   Respondent   Date

_____   _____
Charging Party's Representative   Date   Respondent's Representative   Date

Mediation Settlement Agreement

CHARGE NUMBER:

CHARGING PARTY:

RESPONDENT:

1. In exchange for the promises made by RESPONDENT pursuant to Charge Number ___, CHARGING PARTY agrees not to institute a law suit under [Title VII of the Civil Rights Act of 1964, as amended/the Age Discrimination in Employment Act of 1967, as amended/the Americans with Disabilities Act of 1990, as amended/based on EEOC Charge Number _____].

2. Further, we agree that submission of this agreement to EEOC will constitute a request for closure of EEOC Charge Number _____ and the dually filed charge with a state or local fair employment practices agency.

3. It is understood that this agreement does not constitute an admission by RESPONDENT of any violation of [Title VII of the Civil Rights Act of 1964, as amended; the Age Discrimination in Employment Act of 1967, as amended; and/or the Americans with Disabilities Act of 1990, as amended].

4. RESPONDENT agrees that there shall be no discrimination or retaliation of any kind against CHARGING PARTY as a result of filing this charge or against any person because of opposition to any practice deemed illegal under the ADA, the ADEA or Title VII, as a result of filing this charge, or for giving testimony, assistance or participating in any manner in an investigation, proceeding or a hearing under the aforementioned Acts.

5. This document constitutes a final and complete statement of the agreement between the parties with respect to Charge Number _____.

6. The parties agree that the EEOC is authorized to investigate compliance with this agreement and that this agreement may be specifically enforced in court by the EEOC or the parties and may be used as evidence in a subsequent proceeding in which a breach of this agreement is alleged.

6A. CHARGING PARTY acknowledges that she/he has been advised to consult with an attorney and has been given a reasonable time to consider the agreement before signing.

7. As evidence of a good faith effort to resolve EEOC Charge Number _____, RESPONDENT offers and CHARGING PARTY accepts the following proposal of settlement or (the parties agree):

_____   _____
Respondent   Date

_____   _____
Charging Party   Date

In reliance on the promises made in paragraphs 1 through 7 above, EEOC agrees to terminate its investigation and to not use the above referenced charge as a jurisdictional basis for a civil action under Title VII of the Civil Rights Act of 1964, as amended, the Age Discrimination Act of 1967 as amended, or the Americans with Disabilities Act of 1990, as amended. EEOC does not waive or in any manner limit its right to investigate or seek relief in any other charge, including, but not limited to, a charge filed by a member of the Commission against the Respondent.

On Behalf of the Commission:

_____   _____

                                        Date

Exercise 7:   Calculating Damages

1)   While Ms. Landry's charge is pending at the EEOC, she receives a job offer from Sunflower, Inc. to manage its Abilene, EmLand store. She isn't sure whether she should take it because it pays less in salary ($80,500 versus $95,000) and 401(k) contributions (only 4% versus 5%). Otherwise, the benefits are largely the same. She would, however, have to move from Woodstock to Abilene with her husband and two children. Her start date with Sunflower would be in three weeks.

Should she accept this offer? Why or why not? What known or unknown factors potentially influence her decision?

2)   If Landry was to exhaust her administrative remedies and file suit in federal district court, what damages might she recover if she prevails on her claim and a) takes the job *or* b) declines the job? Obviously, the worst-case scenario for her would be that she is awarded no damages.

Please describe the best-case scenario under these two scenarios. Include a discussion of attorney's fees.

D. SETTLING CLAIMS

Because an estimated ninety-seven percent of all civil cases terminate pre-trial, most often through a negotiated settlement, negotiation is a critical skill.[27] The principles underlying the skill of negotiation are equally relevant in the context of settling claims as they are in mediation.

Before the negotiation begins, you and your client should identify your starting offer, a fallback position, and the point at which you will walk away from negotiations. That planning helps to insulate you from making a bad deal in the heat of the moment. Your preparation should include identifying the rights (known claims and defenses), interests (needs, concerns, abilities), and power of your client and what you perceive to be the rights, interests, and power of your opponent.[28] This requires thoroughly and honestly appraising the strengths and weaknesses of both sides' positions, recognizing that some clients are unsympathetic or lack credibility regardless of how legally strong their claims or defenses are, understanding that "winning" includes consideration of non-monetary factors, such as stress or disruption of business operations and family matters, and assessing a client's continued ability to fund the dispute and pay fees and costs.

Keep in mind that you might know facts that your opponent does not yet know but is likely to discover if the matter continues. Although some of those facts might present your side with an advantage, they are just as likely to present your side with a weakness. You should be careful not to waive the attorney-client privilege by divulging confidential facts during the negotiations.

As the saying goes, "It is easier to catch bees (or flies) with honey than with vinegar." In a mediation or settlement context, you should establish a tone with all of the individuals involved that is appropriate for reaching your goals. During the negotiation, keep in mind that you are there to represent *your client's* best interests—not your own. Try to keep your ego out of the process. Being overly aggressive often hinders the process and hurts your client's interests. It can cause an opponent to terminate the negotiation for emotional reasons before you have even reached the minimum position your client is willing to offer or accept.

You must strive to act ethically and professionally at all times—even if your opponent doesn't. If the parties cannot reach an agreement, it should not be because your conduct was objectionable or because your advice to your client was not sound.

If you are able to settle the case, make sure that you document the terms so they can be memorialized and executed without disagreement or discord. Your client and the opposing party must understand and agree to all of the terms and consequences of the settlement.

---

[27] *See* Jon Rauchway & Mave Gasaway, *Endless Liability? Evaluating whether to settle or litigate private environmental lawsuits at regulated sites,* A.B.A. (Nov. 9, 2018), https://www.americanbar.org/groups/environment_energy_resources/publications/trends/2018-2019/november-december-2018/endless-liability/.

[28] Although many books dedicated to negotiation skills and strategies exist, Stefan Krieger and Richard Neumann include several chapters on the subject in their book *Essential Lawyering Skills,* which also addresses interviewing, counseling, fact analysis, and other important skills. To learn more about identifying the interests, rights, and power of parties in the negotiation context, *see* KRIEGER & NEUMANN, ESSENTIAL LAWYERING SKILLS 298–301 (4th ed. 2011).

Exercise 8:   Settling Claims

EEOC-sponsored mediation has failed between Jan Landry and Daisy Depot. Regardless, you have talked with your opposing counsel and agreed to attempt again to settle the case.

Each side has confidential information, which may have been obtained during initial client interviews in Exercise 1 or provided to you by your instructor in Exercise 5. Over time, you have learned additional confidential information about your clients, which your instructor will provide for you to consider when planning for the settlement negotiations. You also have information necessary to calculate damages provided in Exercise 7, Calculating Damages.

Using this information, identify your starting offer, a fallback position, and the point at which you will walk away from negotiations for your client.

E. THE POSITION STATEMENT

If mediation fails or if the parties decline mediation, the EEOC will investigate the charge. In virtually all instances, the respondent will be asked to file a "position statement" in response to the charge. The EEOC may also ask for specific information such as personnel files, handbooks, disciplinary policies, time-keeping records, or any other documentation that would be relevant to the charge. In some cases, the EEOC may visit the complainant's workplace and interview witnesses.

Although employers are not required to be represented by counsel during the investigation, they should be. Failure to retain counsel can result in insufficient, unnecessary, or excess information being provided, a protracted investigation, and even an expansion of charges.

The defense attorney's role is to investigate, communicate, and counsel. Professionalism requires attorneys to keep an open mind and to investigate the allegations and explanations by: meeting with the client and any witnesses; touring the workplace and assessing the work environment; reviewing personnel files, employment handbooks, job descriptions, recruiting and placement practices; and reviewing the job and performance history of the complainant, decision-makers, witnesses, similarly-situated coworkers, and any alleged "bad actors." Before responding to a charge, the employer's counsel should know *who* made the complained-of decision or was otherwise responsible for the facts alleged, *what* witnesses and documents support the complainant's charge and the company's defense, *when* key events occurred and their relation to each other, *where* key events occurred and where witnesses and documents are located, and *how* key information was transmitted. When drafting a position statement, defense attorneys must be able to support contentions that their clients did not discriminate; a blanket denial will not suffice.

Just as the allegations in the charge can have important repercussions, so too can information provided in response to the charge. Position statements are persuasive documents that deny material allegations directly, present a credible defense to the charge, and request specific relief. Position statements explain how events were shaped by policies, procedures, and job-performance expectations and demonstrate how similarly situated individuals were treated similarly or how unique circumstances led to the charge. They are used by the EEOC during its investigation of the charge and influence whether the EEOC finds reasonable cause to believe that discrimination occurred.[29]

In 2016, in a controversial move, the EEOC began providing charging parties and their counsel with copies of the respondent's position statement and non-confidential documents upon request. Although the EEOC will redact position statements to protect confidential information, respondents must consider that, in addition to the EEOC, the complainant will have access to the information provided. If the complainant chooses to respond to the respondent's position statement, however, the respondent will not receive a copy of the response.

Submitting an accurate and complete position statement has always been important. The EEOC's new process, however, raises the stakes. Respondents must clearly indicate what information is confidential and must submit the information in such a way that the context does not unintentionally reveal confidential information. Moreover, discrepancies between information provided in a position statement and later produced during pretrial discovery could conceivably support a plaintiff's claim that the defendant's justification for its adverse treatment of the plaintiff was pretext.

---

[29] Although position statements are not form documents, they often adhere to a particular structure. The EEOC provides tips for drafting effective position statements at *Effective Position Statements,* EEOC, https://www.eeoc.gov/employers/position_statements.cfm (last visited July 7, 2019). Employment law practitioners often publish tips on their websites and in bar journals and a simple web search can often lead to them.

Exercise 9:   The Position Statement

A sample position statement is attached. Examine its tone, structure, and content and assess whether it is professional and persuasive and how it advances the company's interests. In light of Jan Landry's allegations, what information is the EEOC likely to seek from Daisy Depot if the parties are unable to settle the matter? Keep in mind that the EEOC does not yet know everything that you know; it only has the information Landry provided when filing her charge.

Position Statement

Alaka & Mastrosimone, LLC 2222
Wood Corporate Bay Road
Tina City, EmLand 55551

May 15, 2018

Lindsey A. Kristy, Esq.
Equal Employment Opportunity Commission
1410 Generous Road, Suite 60
Tina City, EmLand 55552

      Re: Paul M. Robinson v. Twilight Corporation Charge No. E-04/08-33269

Dear Ms. Kristy:

We represent Twilight Corporation ("Twilight") in the above-referenced matter and we are in receipt of the charge of discrimination filed by Paul Robinson. On behalf of Twilight, the following is submitted in response to the charge.

I.   SUMMARY

The facts plainly establish that Twilight did not unlawfully discriminate against Mr. Robinson on the basis of his claimed disability or retaliate against him in any way.

Indeed, as evidenced below, Mr. Robinson's discharge resulted from his longstanding, well-documented, and admitted failure to timely arrive at work. Mr. Robinson's position as a system engineer in Twilight's mission-critical Inquiry Response Center required his punctual and consistent attendance so that he could promptly respond to and resolve critical, real-time issues experienced by Twilight's clients around the globe. However, despite repeated counseling and a prior written warning, Mr. Robinson consistently failed to report to work on time, as required. In September 2017, Mr. Robinson's new manager issued him a final warning advising him that he risked termination of his employment if he was unable to get to work on time. However, weeks later Mr. Robinson was late for one shift and just days later was late for another shift—this time requiring his manager to call him and wake him up to inquire whether he would be in that night. Not surprisingly, Mr. Robinson's manager discharged him as a result of his failure to comply with the September 2017 final warning and his historical inability to timely report to work, as required.

II.   PRELIMINARY RESPONSE

A.   The Parties

Twilight is a supplier of healthcare information technology (HIT) solutions and related services. Organizations ranging from single-doctor practices, to hospitals, corporations, and local, regional and national government agencies use *Twilight®* solutions and services to make healthcare safer, more efficient and of higher quality.

Paul Robinson, the complainant, began working for Twilight as an analyst in its mission-critical Inquiry Response Center on March 20, 2013. While Mr. Robinson's analyst position was subsequently reclassified as a "system engineer" position, he continued to work in the Inquiry Response Center until his discharge for tardiness and attendance issues on October 10, 2017.

B. Twilight's Inquiry Response Center.

The Inquiry Response Center ("IRC") operates 24 hours a day, 7 days a week and is committed to providing Twilight's clients with the fastest possible solution or workaround to any "critical issue" that might impair the immediate operation of a Twilight production system. These critical issues are those that impact patient care or cause financial or operational hardship.

The IRC is staffed with two twelve-hour shifts of associates. The day shift begins at 7:00 a.m. and ends at 7:00 p.m. and the night shift begins at 7:00 p.m. and ends at 7:00 a.m. the following day. Associates are expected to arrive at the IRC at least fifteen minutes before the start of their shift in order to participate in the "turnover" discussion where issues that remain unresolved from the preceding shift are discussed and handed off to the next shift.

C. Mr. Robinson's History of Tardiness and Absenteeism was Longstanding.

Mr. Robinson's consistent inability to arrive at work on time in one of Twilight's most important client service departments spanned years of his employment at Twilight. For example, in the last six months of 2014, Mr. Robinson was late for his shift on sixteen separate occasions. And, while these instances of lateness ranged from one to ten minutes, his manager made clear that they affected the nightly turnover process. (A copy of Mr. Robinson's January 2015 semiannual performance evaluation is appended as **Attachment A**).

D. Mr. Robinson's Tardiness Issues Continued into 2015.

Mr. Robinson's continued inability to arrive at work on time necessitated a February 1, 2015, verbal counseling session with his then-manager. During that meeting, his manager highlighted Mr. Robinson's twenty-five incidents of tardiness in 2014 and Mr. Robinson's failure to arrive on time for seven of his scheduled sixteen work days in January 2015 as detailed in the chart below.

2015 Date	Minutes Late for Shift
January 5	22
January 6	11
January 14	10
January 15	3
January 20	90
January 21	6
January 25	23

Based on this serious pattern of tardiness, his manager required Mr. Robinson to "be in the IRC and ready to receive call turnover or available to take calls each scheduled night at your scheduled time" and noted that "ideally" Mr. Robinson should arrive at least ten minutes before the start of his shift. His manager made clear to Mr. Robinson that he needed "to make attendance a top priority and work to reduce and eliminate the pattern that [he had] established."

E. Mr. Robinson was Issued a Written Warning and was Suspended Without Pay for Tardiness.

Failing to improve since his February 2015 counseling session, his manager issued Mr. Robinson a written warning regarding his attendance issues on July 19, 2015. That document detailed nine incidents of tardiness since the February 2015 counseling session, ranging from one to fifty minutes late. In addition to those incidents, Mr. Robinson was also over two hours late for his shift on July 19, 2015. That most recent and egregious example resulted in his manager suspending Mr. Robinson without pay on July 20 and July 21. (A copy of Mr. Robinson's July 2015 Written Warning is appended at **Attachment B**.)

Despite the verbal counseling session, the written warning, and the two-day suspension, Mr. Robinson's attendance issues failed to improve by the issuance of his September 2015 annual performance review. Mr. Robinson, in fact, confirmed his own shortcomings in his self-evaluation when he admitted that "[p]unctuality, while markedly improved, isn't yet to zero incidents." (A copy of Mr. Robinson's September 2015 annual performance evaluation and self-evaluation is appended at **Attachment C**.)

F.   Mr. Robinson's Attendance Problems Resurfaced in 2017.

Mr. Robinson made slight improvements in 2016 but they were not permanent. Whatever improvement 2016 had brought in Mr. Robinson's attendance, such improvements disappeared by July 2017. Twice, on March 16 and 17, Mr. Robinson failed to arrive on time for the turnover call at the start of his shift. On May 2, Mr. Robinson arrived at 10:52 p.m., nearly four hours after the start of his shift. Then, on July 9, Mr. Robinson failed to arrive on time requiring Rachel Bowler, his then-manager, to call him and wake him up at 7:12 p.m. to inquire whether he would be in that night. Mr. Robinson did not arrive until 7:34 p.m. that night. Based on these incidents, Ms. Bowler met with Mr. Robinson on July 18, 2017 to address his tardiness and oversleeping. Mr. Robinson informed Ms. Bowler that he had instituted a "backup plan" (apparently someone else to wake him) and that he would work to make sure it did not happen again. Ms. Bowler made clear to him that he needed to correct this behavior.

Confirming his own failure to consistently arrive at work on time, Mr. Robinson rated himself as failing to meet expectations on his punctuality goals on his July 2017 self-evaluation. Mr. Robinson admitted that punctuality was "one of the main points of emphasis lately" but that he still had "work to do in order to become flawless . . . in this regard." (A copy of Mr. Robinson's July 2017 self-evaluation is appended as **Attachment D**.)

Ms. Bowler's July meeting with Mr. Robinson, like all the other meetings and warnings, did nothing to alter his behavior. Mr. Robinson was five minutes late on August 5, 2017; seventy-five minutes late on August 6, 2017; forty-one minutes late on August 13, 2017 after oversleeping; and fifteen minutes late on September 3, 2017.

Mr. Robinson's admitted failure to arrive at work on time was confirmed during his annual performance evaluation on September 3, 2017 with his new manager, Paul Smith. Mr. Smith rated Mr. Robinson as "did not meet expectations" on his three punctuality goals and reiterated for Mr. Robinson, once again, that his tardiness needed to be corrected. (A copy of Mr. Robinson's 2017 annual performance evaluation is appended as **Attachment E**).

G.   Mr. Robinson was Issued a Final Warning.

Despite the past written warning, the two-day suspension, the self-assessed failing grade on attendance, the counseling sessions with his prior managers, and his September 3, 2017 evaluation with his new manager, Mr. Robinson was late for work again on September 11, 2017. Not only was Mr. Robinson late, but he failed to contact anyone at IRC that he was running late. Instead, Mr. Smith called Mr. Robinson at his home at 7:34 p.m. (34 minutes after the start of his shift) and woke Mr. Robinson up. Mr. Robinson told Mr. Smith that he was not feeling well and that he may be in later in the evening.

Based on Mr. Robinson's failure to arrive at work on time and failure to call in (both violations of his July 2015 written warning), Mr. Smith met with him on September 13, 2017 about his attendance issues and issued Mr. Robinson one last final warning, memorialized in a communication to Mr. Robinson later that day. In that final warning, Mr. Smith summarized Mr. Robinson's poor attendance during 2017 and made clear that should Mr. Robinson "arrive after 7:00 p.m.—this would be deemed unacceptable. No call/no show is deemed unacceptable." Finally, Mr. Smith issued the final warning that "if this behavior continues, you will be subject to further corrective action; *most likely termination of employment*." (A copy of Mr. Smith's communication to Mr. Robinson memorializing his September 13, 2017 final warning is appended as **Attachment F**) (emphasis added).

H. Mr. Robinson was Discharged for Attendance Issues.

Less than three weeks after his final warning, Mr. Robinson called in on October 1, 2017, and informed Twilight than he would be late for his shift that evening due to "tweaking his back." Then, on October 8, 2017, Mr. Robinson was late for his scheduled shift and failed to call in. On October 10, 2017, Mr. Robinson was discharged for his consistent inability to arrive at work on time.

III. MR. ROBINSON'S ALLEGATIONS

In his charge of discrimination Mr. Robinson alleges that:

"In 2012 and throughout my employment thereafter, I requested accommodation for my disability in connection with Twilight's absenteeism, attendance, and job transfer policies."

Twilight flatly denies these allegations. First, Mr. Robinson's charge fails to specify what his claimed disability might be. As such, it is impossible for Twilight to determine whether Mr. Robinson even has a disability within the meaning of the EmLand Human Rights Act ("EHRA") or the Americans with Disabilities Act ("ADA").

Second, while there is uncertainty over Mr. Robinson's claimed status as disabled, there is no uncertainty over the fact that Mr. Robinson never requested any accommodations from Twilight as he was required to do under the EHRA and the ADA. "Where, as here, the disability, resulting limitations, and necessary accommodations, are not open, obvious, and apparent to the employer, as is often the case when mental disabilities are involved, *the initial burden rests primarily upon the employee . . . to specifically identify the disability and resulting limitations, and to suggest the reasonable accommodations*." Wallin v. Minnesota Dept. of Corrections, 153 F.3d 681, 689 (8th Cir. 1998).

A review of Mr. Robinson's employment with Twilight revealed two instances where Mr. Robinson claimed to have particular conditions. First, in May 2013, Mr. Robinson notified Twilight that he was under a doctor's care for allergies. Second, in July 2015, in response to his written warning for his attendance issues, Mr. Robinson provided Twilight with two doctor's notes indicating that he was under a doctor's care for allergies and for depression. (Copies of Mr. Robinson's July 2015 doctor's notes are appended as **Attachment G**.) However, in neither instance did Mr. Robinson request an accommodation from Twilight based on these conditions. Mr. Robinson's failure to suggest to Twilight the accommodations, if any, that he might need to perform the essential functions of his job (i.e., on-time arrival) forecloses his claim as a matter of law. See id. at 471; Rask v. Fresenius Medical Care North America, 509 F.3d 466, 470 (8th Cir. 2017) (finding no duty to accommodate where plaintiff failed provide employer with "the specific limitations that her depression gave rise to").

Moreover, even assuming, *arguendo*, that Mr. Robinson is "disabled," the facts plainly show that he is not a "*qualified* individual with a disability" because he could not perform the essential functions of his job. It is well established that "regular and reliable attendance is a necessary element of most jobs." Spangler v. Federal Home Loan Bank of Des Moines, 278 F.3d 847, 850 (8th Cir. 2012); Rask, 509 F.3d at 469. In fact, "an employee who is unable to come to work on a regular basis [is] unable to satisfy any of the functions of the job in question, much less the essential ones." Spangler, 278 F.3d at 850. By Mr. Robinson's own admission in his self-evaluation, he failed to meet his goals of being "a consistently punctual" associate. This failure, covering over three years of his employment with Twilight in his time-critical job in the Inquiry Response Center, precludes his claim of discrimination.

. . .

Finally, Mr. Robinson alleges that:

"I believe I was retaliated against and discharged because of my disability."

Twilight flatly denies Mr. Robinson's allegation that his discharge was based on anything other than his well-documented, longstanding, and admitted attendance issues. Mr. Robinson's job in the IRC required not only his on-time arrival by 7:00 but an early arrival by 6:45 p.m. to discuss any issues left over by the off-going shift. The very nature of the IRC's work (addressing critical, real-time issues Twilight's clients are experiencing with Twilight's software solutions) demands that its staff be on time and ready to respond and resolve these immediate concerns at the start of their shift.

During the course of three years, Mr. Robinson proved time and again that he was simply unable or unwilling to regularly arrive at Twilight at his required work time despite Twilight's best efforts to get Mr. Robinson to improve his performance. The many counseling sessions with his managers failed to correct this problem. The move from the day shift to the night shift failed to correct this problem. The offer of short-term disability leave failed to correct this problem. The written warning failed to correct this problem. The offer to conference call into the turnover call failed to correct this problem. The years of "does not meet expectations" ratings on his punctuality goals failed to correct this problem. Repeated warnings from three different managers failed to correct this problem. The final warning issued by his new manager failed to correct this problem. Even Mr. Robinson's apparent use of multiple alarm clocks and arranging for "backup" people to wake him up failed to correct this problem. Finally, after years of warnings from Twilight and repeated failures by Mr. Robinson, Twilight discharged Mr. Robinson not because of any claimed disability but because of his own admitted failure to arrive at work on time.

In fact, Mr. Robinson is not the only IRC associate who has been disciplined or discharged for attendance and timeliness issues. Like Mr. Robinson, three other non-disabled IRC associates were issued written warnings in 2017 for their failure to arrive at work on time or for their failure to notify their supervisor when they would not be at work. (**Confidential** copies of these written warning are appended as **Attachment H**.) Additionally, another nondisabled IRC associate was discharged on December 15, 2016 when she was over 30 minutes late for her December 8, 2017 shift and was a "no call/no show" for her December 9, 2017 shift. Twilight's discipline and discharge of these other non-disabled associates for the same conduct in which Mr. Robinson engaged conclusively shows that it did not take such action against Mr. Robinson because of any disability that he might have.

IV. CONCLUSION

The evidence conclusively demonstrates that Twilight did not unlawfully discriminate against Mr. Robinson on the basis of his claimed disability or retaliate against him in violation of any federal, state, or local law. Accordingly, Mr. Robinson's charge must be dismissed.

Responses to your standard interrogatories are included herein and in the attachments. If you have any questions, or if you need any additional information with which to complete your investigation, please let me know.

Very truly yours,

T.R. Schwein

T.R. Schwein

TRS:jpm

List of Attachments

A.   Mr. Robinson's January 2015 semi-annual performance evaluation

B.   Mr. Robinson's July 2015 written warning

C.   Mrs. Robinson's September 2015 annual performance evaluation and self-evaluation

D.   Mr. Robinson's July 2017 self-evaluation

E.   Mr. Robinson's 2017 annual performance evaluation

F.   Mr. Smith's communication to Mr. Robinson memorializing his September 13, 2017 final warning

G.   Mr. Robinson's July 2015 doctor's notes

H.   **Confidential** 2017 written warnings to Mr. Robinson's coworkers.

F. EXHAUSTION OF ADMINISTRATIVE REMEDIES

CLOSING OUT THE CHARGE AND FILING SUIT[30]

The administrative process concludes with the EEOC advising the parties of its conclusion regarding the charge and issuing a "right to sue." The closing documents differ depending on the EEOC's findings.[31] If, after completing its investigation, the EEOC finds reasonable cause, it will attempt to resolve the matter though its conciliation process. If conciliation fails, the EEOC may file suit against respondent or issue the complainant a Notice of Suit Rights.

If the EEOC is unable to find reasonable cause that discrimination occurred, it will issue a Dismissal and Notice of Rights to the complainant informing her that she has ninety days to file suit in federal court. Respondent also receives a copy of this Notice.

In some cases, a complainant may not wish to wait for the EEOC to complete its investigation before filing suit or the EEOC is unable to complete its investigation of the charge within the statutorily mandated period. In such cases, the complainant may request a Right to Sue. Depending on how much time has passed since the charge was filed and whether the agency's investigations are backlogged, the agency may issue the Right to Sue.

If the complainant wishes to pursue her claim against the company, the complainant has ninety days to file a complaint in federal court once the EEOC has closed its file. As noted earlier, the claims made in the complaint are limited in scope to those found in the charge. Although a "no cause" finding does not preclude a complainant from suing, the parties are reminded of their obligations under the rules of professional responsibility and civil procedure to refrain from asserting frivolous claims or defenses and of their duties to sufficiently investigate all assertions made to the court.

In a unanimous opinion issued in June 2019, the Supreme Court held that Title VII's exhaustion requirements are mandatory claim-processing rules but are not jurisdictional.[32] The significance of this distinction is that courts must enforce the rules if they are properly raised, "[b]ut an objection based on a mandatory claim-processing rule may be forfeited 'if the party asserting the rule waits too long to raise the point.' "[33] Thus, if a plaintiff raises a claim in federal court that was not raised at the EEOC, the defendant waives the opportunity to dismiss the claim if it fails to timely raise the issue.[34]

The exhaustion requirements for claims brought under the ADEA are different from those of Title VII in one significant respect. They can also vary under state law. Knowing exhaustion requirements is an essential aspect of an attorney's professional obligations.

---

[30]   For further information, including exceptions to the general information provided here, *see Filing a Lawsuit*, EEOC, https:// www.eeoc.gov/employees/lawsuit.cfm (last visited July 7, 2019).

[31]   Examples of EEOC dismissal notices referred to within this text are provided on the following pages for your information.

[32]   Fort Bend Cty. v. Davis, 587 U.S. ___, 139 S.Ct. 1843 (2019).

[33]   *Id*. at 1849 (internal citations omitted).

[34]   *Id*.

Exercise 10: Exhaustion of Administrative Remedies

1)   The previous text states that ADEA administrative exhaustion requirements differ from those of Title VII. In what way are they different?

2)   The administrative process varies from state to state. Can you find the procedural requirements in your state? How do they differ from the EEOC process?

U.S. EQUAL EMPLOYMENT OPPORTUNITY COMMISSION
NOTICE OF RIGHT TO SUE
(CONCILIATION FAILURE)

To:	Manuel Martinez 11111 Square Drive Southdown, MI 48888	From:	Detroit Field Office 477 Michigan Avenue Room 865 Detroit, MI

☐ On behalf of person(s) aggrieved whose identity is
CONFIDENTIAL (29 CFR § 1601.7(a))

EEOC Charge No.	EEOC Representative S.T. Weaver, Investigator	Telephone No.
471-2009-02744		(313) 313-3113

TO THE PERSON AGGRIEVED:

This notice concludes the EEOC's processing of the above-numbered charge. The EEOC found reasonable cause to believe that violations of the statute(s) occurred with respect to some or all of the matters alleged in the charge but could not obtain a settlement with the Respondent that would provide relief for you. In addition, the EEOC has decided that it will not bring suit against the Respondent at this time based on this charge and will close its file in this case. This does not mean that the EEOC is certifying that the Respondent is in compliance with the law, or that the EEOC will not sue the Respondent later or intervene later in your lawsuit if you decide to sue on your own behalf.

- NOTICE OF SUIT RIGHTS -
(See the additional information attached to this form)

Title VII, the Americans with Disabilities Act, the Genetic Information Nondiscrimination Act, or the Age Discrimination in Employment Act: This will be the only notice of dismissal and of your right to sue that we will send you. You may file a lawsuit against the respondent(s) under federal law based on this charge in federal or state court. Your lawsuit **must be filed WITHIN 90 DAYS of your receipt of this notice**; or your right to sue based on this charge will be lost. (The time limit for filing based on a claim under state law may be different.)

Equal Pay Act (EPA): EPA suits must be filed in federal or state court within 2 years (3 years for willful violations) of the alleged EPA underpayment. This means that **backpay due for any violations that occurred more than 2 years (3 years) before you file suit may not be collectible.**

If you file suit, based on this charge, please send a copy of your court complaint to this office.

On behalf of the Commission

Web N. Smithe   9/27/10

Enclosure(s)

Web N. Smithe   (Date Mailed)
Acting District Director

cc: Brian Zulo   William L. Horth
Director of Human Resources   10th Floor Columbria Center
Company, INC.   101 W. Big Beaver Rd.
66661 Bunett   Waverly, MI 88080
Waverly, MI 88080

U.S. EQUAL EMPLOYMENT OPPORTUNITY COMMISSION
DISMISSAL AND NOTICE OF RIGHTS

To:	Manuel Martinez 11111 Square Drive Southdown, MI 48888	From:	Detroit Field Office 477 Michigan Avenue Room 865 Detroit, MI

☐ On behalf of person(s) aggrieved whose identity is CONFIDENTIAL (29 CFR § 1601.7(a))

EEOC Charge No.	EEOC Representative **S.T. Weaver,** **Investigator**	Telephone No.
281-2004-03088		(313) 313-3113

THE EEOC IS CLOSING ITS FILE ON THIS CHARGE FOR THE FOLLOWING REASON:

☐ The facts alleged in the charge fail to state a claim under any of the statutes enforced by the EEOC.

☐ Your allegations did not involve a disability as defined by the Americans with Disabilities Act

☐ The Respondent employs less that the required number of employees or is not otherwise covered by the statutes

☐ Your charge was not timely filed with the EEOC; in other words, you waited too long after the date(s) of alleged discrimination to file your charge.

☐ Having been given 30 days in which to respond, you failed to provide information, failed to appear or be available for interviews/conferences, or otherwise failed to cooperate to the extend that it was not possible to resolve your charge.

☐ While reasonable efforts were made to locate you, we were not able to do so.

☐ You were given 30 days to accept a reasonable settlement offer that affords full relief for the harm you alleged.

☒ The EEOC issues the following determination: Based upon its investigation, the EEOC is unable to conclude that the information obtained establishes violations of the statutes. This does not certify that the respondent is in compliance with the statutes. No finding is made as to any other issues that might be construed as having been raised in this charge.

☐ The EEOC has accepted the findings of the state or local fair employment practices agency that investigated this charge.

☐ Other (*briefly state*)

- NOTICE OF SUIT RIGHTS -
(See the additional information attached to this form)

Title VII, the Americans with Disabilities Act, the Genetic Information Nondiscrimination Act, or the Age Discrimination in Employment Act: This will be the only notice of dismissal and of your right to sue that we will send you. You may file a lawsuit against the respondent(s) under federal law based on this charge in federal or state court. Your lawsuit **must be filed WITHIN 90 DAYS of your receipt of this notice**; or your right to sue based on this charge will be lost. (The time limit for filing based on a claim under state law may be different.)

Equal Pay Act (EPA): EPA suits must be filed in federal or state court within 2 years (3 years for willful violations) of the alleged EPA underpayment. This means that **backpay due for any violations that occurred more than 2 years (3 years)** before you file suit may **not be collectible.**

On behalf of the Commission

Web N. Smithe   9/27/04

Enclosure(s)	Web N. Smithe Acting District Director	(Date Mailed)

cc: Brian Zulo   William L. Horth
      Director of Human Resources   10th Floor Columbia Center
      Company, INC.   101 W. Big Beaver Rd.
      66661 Bunett, Waverly, MI 88080   Waverly, MI 88080

U.S. EQUAL EMPLOYMENT OPPORTUNITY COMMISSION
NOTICE OF RIGHT TO SUE (*ISSUED ON REQUEST*)

To:	Manuel Martinez 11111 Square Drive Southdown, MI 48888	From:	Detroit Field Office 477 Michigan Avenue Room 865 Detroit, MI

☐ On behalf of person(s) aggrieved whose identity is
CONFIDENTIAL (29 CFR § 1601.7(a))

EEOC Charge No.	EEOC Representative **S.T. Weaver,**	Telephone No.
420-2017-00377	**Investigator**	**(313) 313-3113**

NOTICE TO THE PERSON AGGRIEVED:

Title VII of the Civil Rights Act of 1964, the Americans with Disabilities Act (ADA), or the Genetic Information Nondiscrimination Act (GINA): This is your Notice of Right to Sue, issued under Title VII, the ADA or GINA based on the above-numbered charge. It has been issued at your request. Your lawsuit under Title VII, the ADA or GINA **must be filed in a federal or state court WITHIN 90 DAYS of your receipt of this notice**; or your right to sue based on this charge will be lost. (The time limit for filing suit based on a claim under state law may be different.)

☒ More than 180 days have passed since the filing of this charge.

☐ Less than 180 days have passed since the filing of this charge, but I have determined that it is unlikely that the EEOC will be able to complete its administrative process within 180 days from the filing of this charge.

☒ The EEOC is terminating its processing of this charge.

☐ The EEOC will continue to process this charge.

Age Discrimination in Employment Act (ADEA): You may sue under the ADEA at any time from 60 days after the charge was filed until 90 days after you receive notice that we have completed action on the charge. In this regard, the paragraph marked below applies to your case:

☐ The EEOC is closing your case. Therefore, your lawsuit under the ADEA **must be filed in federal or state court WITHIN 90 DAYS of your receipt of this Notice.** Otherwise, your right to sue based on the above-numbered charge will be lost.

☐ The EEOC is continuing its handling of your ADEA case. However, if 60 days have passed since the filing of the charge, you may file suit in federal or state court under the ADEA at this time.

Equal Pay Act (EPA): You already have the right to sue under the EPA (filing an EEOC charge is not required). EPA suits must be brought in federal or state court within 2 years (3 years for willful violations) of the alleged EPA underpayment. This means that backpay due for any violations that occurred more than 2 years (3 years) before you file suit may not be collectible.

If you file suit, based on this charge, please send a copy of your court complaint to this office.

On behalf of the Commission

Web N. Smithe   9/27/17

Enclosure(s)   Web N. Smithe   (Date Mailed)
                                Acting District Director

cc: Brian Zulo   William L. Horth
        Director of Human Resources   10th Floor Columbia Center
        Company, INC.   101 W. Big Beaver Rd.
        66661 Bunett, Waverly, MI 88080   Waverly, MI 88080

CHAPTER THREE

WAGES, HOURS, AND CONDITIONS OF WORK

I. INTRODUCTION TO WAGES, HOURS AND CONDITIONS OF WORK

In 1938, after an era of excessive work hours, low pay, and oppressive child labor, Congress enacted the Fair Labor Standards Act (FLSA) to establish standards for minimum wages, overtime pay, recordkeeping, and child labor. Enforced by the U.S. Department of Labor, the FLSA has a broad reach; it affects full- and part-time workers in the private sector and in federal, state, and local governments, although it exempts certain industries, occupations, and workers from its provisions.

State wage and hour laws can also affect pay and working conditions by filling gaps in the federal law, requiring higher minimum wages, and providing greater protections or benefits for the workers within their state. State departments of labor typically enforce state wage and hour laws.

Lawyers can often save significant expense for their clients and significant time for themselves—not to mention potential liability—by familiarizing themselves with the extensive information provided by agency websites. The Department of Labor's website[1] offers access to information about the laws it enforces, identifies wage and hour topics that federal law does not cover, and provides helpful pathways for finding some state laws. For example, the Department of Labor's Wage and Hour Division (WHD) portal provides a link to an interactive map with the minimum wages for each state, as well as "toolkits" that answer frequently asked questions about federal labor standards, including those relating to the FLSA and the Family and Medical Leave Act (FMLA).

A. RESEARCHING WAGE AND HOUR LAW

This chapter contains a small representation of the issues that frequently arise regarding wage and hour laws. Nonetheless, it is intended to demonstrate the breadth and complexity of wage and hour law.

Although cases interpreting statutes and regulations are important, they should not be your starting point. The goal of the following exercises is to familiarize you with important federal and state laws and regulations, as well as agency websites that provide inroads into accessing and understanding that law. These websites should be the starting point for your research.

You can also use the Bloomberg Law State Laws Charter Builder or its Wage and Hour Reporter, web searches, and other research resources—digital or in books—to further hone your research skills. You should keep in mind, however, that summaries of the law are not the law; they are secondary sources that can provide an overview of the law and lead you to the primary source. As with any heavily regulated area of the law, it is important to locate and read the state and federal wage and hour statutes themselves, as well as any relevant regulations and guidance documents. This is not an area where you always "know a violation when you see it" and significant pitfalls exist.

---

[1]   DEP'T OF LABOR, www.dol.gov (last visited July 7, 2019).

You may find it instructive to attempt to resolve the following research problems without first accessing federal or state department of labor websites. By comparing the time it takes to locate relevant information, you may further develop your instincts for best research practices.

Exercise 11:   What Can I Find on the U.S. Department of Labor Website?

This exercise is designed to familiarize you with important resources for counseling employers and workers on wage and hour issues. Although it is focused on the federal department of labor's website, www.dol.gov, similar information can often be found at the state level. Keep in mind that state law often addresses wage and hour issues that federal law does not or addresses them in similar but not identical ways. For example, many states have fewer exemptions than the FLSA.

Please consider the following questions:

1) Access the "Topics" tab at the top of the DOL's home page.

   a) How many topics are listed?

   b) What key topics are identified?

   c) Does the Federal Office of Workers' Compensation Programs provide wage-replacement or other benefits for employees who are injured while working for a private employer?

   d) If you were injured while working at a law firm in your home state, where would you file for workers' compensation benefits?

   e) What pathway would you follow to determine whether employers are required to provide meal periods or rest breaks under the Fair Labor Standards Act's (FLSA)?

2) Access the Wage and Hour Division (WHD) home page using the "Agencies" tab at the top of the home page.
   a) What categories of information can you access from the WHD home page?

   b) On what topics can you obtain information in the "popular pages" section?

   c) What pathway would you follow to obtain forms relating to the Family and Medical Leave Act?

   d) What pathway would you follow to obtain information regarding what constitutes "working time" or "hours worked" under the FLSA?

3) From the DOL's home page, what pathway would you take to find information regarding child labor?

Exercise 12: Meal Breaks and Rest Periods

An attorney recently contacted Penelope Duquette, Daisy Depot's Vice President of Human Resources, purporting to represent employees in many states in a potential class action lawsuit regarding the company's alleged failure to provide employees with required meal breaks and rest periods. Although Ms. Duquette thinks the attorney is bluffing, she is seeking counsel because she has heard that employees in several states have been grumbling about their wages and working conditions.

Using federal *and* state departments of labor websites as starting points, please answer the following questions and cite the law or other source upon which your answers are based.

1) Does federal law require employers to provide meal breaks and/or rest periods to its employees?

2) Is Daisy Depot required to give meal breaks and/or rest periods under the laws of the state(s) identified by your instructor?

3) Is Daisy Depot required to compensate employees for the time they would spend on meal breaks or rest periods?

Exercise 13: Terminating the Employment Relationship/Deductions from Wages

Blew Right Inn is a well-known chain hotel. Over the last year, George Mitchell, the general manager of one of its larger hotels, began to suspect that an employee had been stealing. After making subtle inquiries, Mitchell determined that if he had a problem, it was most likely with a night-shift worker. About six months ago, he alerted all of his employees that he was installing new surveillance cameras for their protection.[2] While it is true Mitchell cares about his employees' well-being, his primary purpose in installing the new cameras was to catch a thief.

After watching the tapes, Mitchell suspected that the culprit was his night-shift desk clerk, David Clark. Several times, Mitchell observed Clark on tape handling cash in an unauthorized way and going into the safe for no apparent reason. Each time that happened, the hotel's cash receipts were off.

About six weeks ago, Blew Right Inn's security guard stopped Clark one morning when Clark was headed home. Clark had $200 in his coat pocket and no explanation regarding why he was carrying such a large sum. Mitchell fired Clark on the spot. Mitchell told Clark that he would get his final paycheck after he made restitution for the amount he stole, which Mitchell calculated to be about $3,000, including the $200 he had in his pocket that morning.

Clark demanded to be paid immediately and reminded Mitchell that he was not convicted of any crime. Mitchell refused, called him a thief, and told him to expect the police to come knocking at his door. After Mitchell refused, Clark left but he sent Mitchell an email the next day demanding the wages he had not been paid. Mitchell ignored the email but contacted the police department to file a report concerning the theft.

Mitchell has just received a notice from the state department of labor informing him that the department had commenced an investigation regarding whether he had violated the state's wage laws for withholding Clark's final paycheck. The letter suggested that the hotel could be on the hook for the wages and potential penalties, which would substantially increase the amount Blew Right Inn owed Clark. Mitchell has consulted with his Human Resource Manager, who told him she would check with you.

Did Mitchell have the right to withhold Clark's final wages under state law?

---

[2] Although this exercise may present privacy issues, they are beyond the scope of the exercise unless otherwise instructed.

B. CHILD LABOR—AGES, HOURS, AND OCCUPATIONS
(NON-AGRICULTURAL)

There was a time in this country when young children routinely worked legally. As industry grew in the period following the Civil War, children, often as young as 10 years old but sometimes much younger, labored. They worked not only in industrial settings but also in retail stores, on the streets, on farms, and in home-based industries.[3]

Until Congress passed the Fair Labor Standards Act in 1938, children were widely employed for long hours and under dangerous conditions in coal mines, fabric and steel mills, canneries, and agriculture, for example. Although laws attempting to curtail such practices were contemplated, they were routinely resisted and, if passed, struck down.[4] Today, the FLSA—and some state laws—regulate the ages, hours, and occupations of workers under the age of eighteen. In contrast to pre-FLSA working conditions, these laws seek to ensure that when young people work, the work is safe and does not jeopardize their health, well-being, or educational opportunities. The minimum wage, overtime, health and safety, and anti-discrimination laws that apply to adults also apply to minors, unless specific exemptions exist. As in other areas of the law, if state law provides greater protections to minors, the state law controls.

The Wage and Hour Division (WHD) of the DOL administers and enforces the FLSA and investigates alleged violations of minimum wage, overtime, and child labor laws, while the state departments of labor administer and enforce their own laws. Because state law can be stricter or provide protections not found in federal law, alleged violations of child-labor laws can result in investigations by both federal and state agencies. Violations of federal child-labor laws include civil money penalties, injunctive relief, and criminal sanctions in the case of willful violations.

According to WHD statistics, 1,600 minors working in violation of child-labor laws were identified in 2017, with close to five hundred employed in hazardous occupations.[5] These numbers are significantly lower than just ten years earlier. In 2007, the DOL identified 4,672 minors working in violation of child-labor laws and 1,000 minors working in hazardous occupations.[6] This change may have more to do with a decrease in the number of inspectors investigating alleged child-labor violations than with an actual decrease in child-labor violations.[7] DOL enforcement actions demonstrate, however, that child-labor violations occur across different industrial sectors and employers that violate the law can face stiff penalties.[8]

---

[3]   Michael Schuman, *History of Child Labor in the United States—Part 1: Little Children Working*, BUREAU OF LABOR STATS. (Jan. 2017), https://www.bls.gov/opub/mlr/2017/article/history-of-child-labor-in-the-united-states-part-1.htm.

[4]   *See generally* Michael Schuman, *History of Child Labor in the United States—Part 2: The Reform Movement*, BUREAU OF LABOR STATS. (Jan. 2017), https://www.bls.gov/opub/mlr/2017/article/history-of-child-labor-in-the-united-states-part-2-the-reform-movement.htm.

[5]   *See Fiscal Year Data for WHD*, DEP'T OF LABOR, https://www.dol.gov/whd/data/datatables.htm (last visited July 7, 2019) (providing aggregate yearly enforcement data).

[6]   *See id.*

[7]   A 2014 article exploring child-labor noted that personnel cutbacks at the state and federal level and the loosening of some child-labor restrictions have resulted in decreased enforcement activities. *See* Alana Semuels, *How Common is Child Labor in the U.S.?*, THE ATLANTIC (Dec. 15, 2014), https://www.theatlantic.com/business/archive/2014/12/how-common-is-chid-labor-in-the-us/383687/.

[8]   *See, e.g.,* Acosta v. Paragon Contractors Corp., 884 F.3d. 1225 (10th Cir. 2018) (upholding a compensatory fine of $200,000 for violating an earlier order prohibiting children from working as pecan pickers); USDL 18–0254 News Release, *U.S. Department of Labor Investigation Results in Wendy's Franchisee Paying $258,249 Penalty After Child Labor Violations At 53 Michigan Restaurants*, 2018 WL 915871 (Feb. 16, 2018) (violations included permitting minors to operate deep fryers and work longer hours than permitted); USDL 17–1647 News Release, *Pennsylvania Manufacturer to Pay $377,144 to 47 Employees Following Investigation by U.S. Department of Labor*, 2017 WL 6524638 (Dec. 21, 2017) (fines included over $30,000 for permitting employees sixteen and younger to engage in hazardous manufacturing activities, including operating circular saws and drills).

OVERVIEW OF THE LAW

In addition to setting federal minimum wage, overtime pay, and employers' record-keeping responsibilities, the FLSA prohibits the use of "oppressive child labor" and the shipment or delivery of goods that employ oppressive child labor[9]—the so-called "hot goods" provision.[10] With some exceptions, the Act defines "oppressive child labor" as the employment of individuals under the age of sixteen in any occupation, or the employment of individuals between the ages of sixteen and eighteen "in any occupation which the Secretary of Labor shall find and by order declare to be particularly hazardous for the employment of children between such ages or detrimental to their health or well-being . . . ."[11] Important distinctions are made between agricultural and non-agricultural employment,[12] and the "act includes several exemptions, . . . that create a complex set of thresholds that depend on the child's age, local school hours, the nature of the work (e.g., occupation, industry, and work environment), parental involvement in the child's employment, and other factors."[13]

While the FLSA specifically identifies a few agricultural and non-agricultural occupations that may be exempted from the child labor prohibitions under certain conditions, you must consult the regulations to determine when minors may work and what occupations the Secretary of Labor has deemed to be hazardous. These can be found in 29 C.F.R. § 570, *et. seq.* For example:

- Subpart C regulates the working hours and occupations of minors between fourteen and sixteen-years-old;

- Subpart E defines the "hazardous orders," those being "occupations particularly hazardous for the employment of minors between 16 and 18 years of age or detrimental to their health or well-being";[14] and

- Subpart E-1 identifies "occupations in agriculture particularly hazardous for the employment of children below the age of 16."[15]

Because child-labor regulations restrict the hours that minors can work and the activities in which they may engage, employment lawyers must become familiar with the details of the law. The brief overview of the law contained in this chapter cannot begin to provide the information that work experience provides. The ability to quickly access relevant law is a key skill. Not only is it unlikely that anyone can commit this complicated regulatory scheme to memory, the law periodically changes, as well. The WHD child-labor resources webpage provides an excellent overview of the law[16] but, as always, the actual text of the law or regulation must be reviewed. Web pages are often not updated as quickly as the law changes.

Advising clients in a field that is constantly in flux is one of the challenges employment lawyers face. This is particularly true in the area of wages and hours. For example, in 2016, the DOL changed several aspects of the rules classifying employees for overtime purposes in order to enable more workers to be eligible for overtime pay. The rule was stayed during litigation challenging the changes and eventually invalidated. After the DOL under the Trump administration abandoned its

---

[9]   29 U.S.C. §§ 212(a), (c) (2012).

[10]   For more information regarding the FLSA's "hot goods" provisions, *see Fact Sheet #80: The Prohibition against Shipment of "Hot Goods" Under the Fair Labor Standards Act*, DEP'T OF LABOR, https://www.dol.gov/whd/regs/compliance/whdfs80.pdf (last visited Jul. 7, 2019).

[11]   29 U.S.C. § 203(*l*).

[12]   *See id.* § 213(c)(1)–(2), (4)(a)–(4)(b). Exceptions to the child labor laws also exist for individuals employed in the performance arts. *See id.* § 213(c)(3).

[13]   Sarah A. Donovan & Jon O. Shimabukuro, *Summary, The Fair Labor Standards Act (FLSA) Child Labor Provisions*, CONG. RESEARCH SERV. (June 29, 2016), https://fas.org/sgp/crs/misc/R44548.pdf. *See also* 29 U.S.C. § 213(c).

[14]   *See* 29 C.F.R. §§ 570.50–.68 (2018).

[15]   *See id.* §§ 570.70–.72.

[16]   From the "Topics" tab on the DOL's homepage, www.dol.gov, choose "Youth and Labor."

defense of the final rule, it proposed new rules which would extend the overtime protections, but to fewer employees than the 2016 rule change it replaced.[17] The DOL issued the new overtime rules on September 27, 2019 with an effective date of January 1, 2020.[18]

Additionally, in May 2018, President Trump's Task Force on Apprenticeship Expansion submitted a report with a strategy for expanding youth apprenticeship programs. Recommendations included in the proposed new rules include relaxing some of the Hazardous Orders, including those relating to the operation of power-hoisted lifts in the health care industry.[19] Because some of those recommendations will be controversial, it is impossible to predict at this point whether or how the Hazardous Orders will change. Thus, employment lawyers must advise clients on current law, while keeping an eye out for proposed changes, to ensure they competently and ethically advise their clients.

---

[17] *See* News Release 19-0474-NAT, *U.S. Department of Labor's Overtime Proposal Open for Public Comment*, DEP'T OF LABOR (Mar. 22, 2019), https://www.dol.gov/newsroom/releases/whd/whd20190322; Jeff Stein, *Trump Administration Releases New Rules on Overtime Pay*, WASH. POST (Mar. 7, 2019).

[18] Defining and Delimiting the Exemptions for Executive, Administrative, Professional, Outside Sales and Computer Employees, 84 Fed. Reg. 51230 (Sept. 27, 2019) (to be codified at 29 C.F.R. pt. 541).

[19] Expanding Employment, Training, and Apprenticeship Opportunities for 16- and 17-Year-Olds in Health Care Occupations Under the Fair Labor Standards Act, 83 Fed. Reg. 48,737 (proposed Sept. 27, 2018) (to be codified at 29 C.F.R. § 570.58).

Exercise 14: Child Labor—Ages, Hours, and Occupations (Non-Agricultural)

You have received the following email message from Andy Bernard, one of Daisy Depot's store managers. Use the DOL's "Labor and Youth" portal as a starting point.

What is your advice? Do you have all of the information necessary to advise him? If not, how would you suggest obtaining it?

* * *

This is Andy Bernard, the new store manager of Daisy Depot's Paxico, EmLand store. Penelope Duquette suggested that I contact you. We recently completed a DOL audit, which was a new experience for me. I think the audit went well but as one of the investigators was leaving, she asked me how old some of our teenaged employees are. The teenagers she was asking about were unloading delivery vans, unpacking inventory, and stocking shelves. I told the investigator that I'm not sure how old the kids are because the stockers range in age from 15–18 years old. Well, the investigator told me that I had better find out because she intended to come back and check on the ages, duties, and working hours of all minor employees working in Daisy Depot's Paxico store.

Because of the shortage of labor in Paxico, I regularly employ high school students to be "stockers." In addition to helping with unpacking boxes and stocking shelves, they sometimes help unload delivery vans, load the freight elevator, deliver the new products to the basement storeroom via the freight elevator, and use the compressor to flatten and stack the empty cardboard boxes. Once in a great while, a particularly resourceful stocker might move inventory with a forklift.

I'm pretty sure I'm on top of the child labor laws but I'd like to know whether I have anything to worry about here. Although I know you will have to check state law eventually too, right now I just want to know whether federal law prohibits minors from performing those tasks. The feds are the ones who seem to be all riled up. I also want to double check what the working hour restrictions are.

Thanks,
Andy

Andrew Bernard
Daisy Depot
1234 Depot Way
Paxico, EmLand 66699
555-555-0987

II. COUNSELING EMPLOYERS: THE INTERSECTION OF WAGE AND HOUR LAW AND THE FAMILY MEDICAL LEAVE ACT

Few aspects of employment law are as complex as those arising from the interplay of laws providing benefits for ill, injured, or disabled employees. If an employee acquires an occupational disease or sustains losses resulting from injuries arising out of and in the course of employment, the employee may be eligible for benefits under state workers' compensation laws. If an employee needs time off because of a serious injury or illness, the employee may be entitled to family and medical leave. If an employee has a physical or mental disability, the employee may be entitled to workplace accommodations and protected from discrimination by the Americans with Disabilities Act. Depending on the circumstances, workers' compensation laws, the Family and Medical Leave Act, the Americans with Disabilities Act or any combination of those laws may apply despite differences in their purpose, scope, and coverage.

Although it is in the employer's best interest to have a healthy workforce, personnel needs, economic realities, and workplace dynamics complicate the ability to address illness, injury, and disability in the workplace. Additionally, the fact that other workers may be called upon to assume some or all of the duties of ill, injured, or disabled employees can cause strain and resentment in the workforce and additional costs for employers. An employee's statutory right to privacy may limit an employer's ability to explain to other affected employees why they are assuming these additional responsibilities. For an employee, the need to care for oneself can be complicated by the lack of adequate health care coverage or paid time off.

Although workers' compensation laws, the FMLA, and the ADA can overlap, these laws are enforced by different agencies. As a result, employees seeking redress under these laws might have to navigate different procedural requirements. For example, the WHD administers the FMLA, although employees who believe that their FMLA rights have been violated have a choice of filing a complaint at the DOL or a private lawsuit against their employer. The WHD also administers workers' compensation benefits for federal employees while state workers' compensation agencies administer the benefits for employees of state or local government agencies and private employers. Finally, the EEOC enforces the ADA and workers who believe that they have claims under that law must exhaust administrative remedies by first filing a charge with that agency.

An additional layer of complexity exists: How do wage and hour laws interact with leave entitlements when an employee is absent during part of a workday? Put another way, are employees entitled to be paid for time they are not working because of accommodations made for illness, injury, or disability?

If you have accessed the DOL's website for problems arising under the FLSA, you are acquainted with the guidance, fact sheets, and other important reference information that can be found there. You should also be aware that the DOL will issue opinion letters in response to queries made by attorneys posing specific questions they and their clients are grappling with. These opinion letters provide insight into how the agency would apply the law if a complaint raising the facts alleged were filed. Practicing attorneys should keep abreast of DOL guidance and review previously issued guidance letters when faced with unique situations. These are available on the DOL's website.

OVERVIEW OF THE LAW

The FLSA requires that employees receive at least a minimum wage for all hours worked and time-and-a-half, based on their regular rate of pay, for all hours worked over forty hours in a workweek, unless they are "exempt" from the overtime provisions of the FLSA, the minimum wage provisions, or both.[20] Although that requirement appears fairly straightforward, employers may struggle with how to define terms like "hours worked" and "regular rate of pay," and may seek counsel on which of their employees are "exempt." Defining these concepts has been additionally complicated by amendments to the law and the fact that each of these concepts has been litigated.

The FLSA defines the term "employ" as "to suffer or permit to work,"[21] but does not further define "work." Recognizing that the "amount of money an employee should receive cannot be determined without knowing the number of hours worked," the DOL devotes an entire section of its regulations to discussing "the principles involved in determining what constitutes working time."[22] Although acknowledging that "ultimate decisions on interpretations of the act are made by the courts," the DOL "provide[s] a 'practical guide for employers and employees as to how the office representing the public interest in its enforcement will seek to apply it.' "[23]

Unlike the FLSA, the FMLA is not directly concerned with "working time." Instead, the FMLA is focused on providing most eligible employees with at least twelve workweeks of protected leave from work in a twelve-month period to address specified family and medical needs, including:

- The birth of a child and to care for the newborn child within one year of birth;

- The placement with the employee of a child for adoption or foster care and to care for the newly placed child within one year of placement;

- To care for the employee's spouse, child, or parent who has a serious health condition;

- A serious health condition that makes the employee unable to perform the essential functions of his or her job;

- Any qualifying exigency arising out of the fact that the employee's spouse, son, daughter, or parent is a covered military member on "covered active duty;" or

- Twenty-six workweeks of leave during a single twelve-month period to care for a covered servicemember with a serious injury or illness if the eligible employee is the servicemember's spouse, son, daughter, parent, or next of kin (military caregiver leave).[24]

Prior to the FMLA, workers who found themselves needing leave for any of the above reasons faced the possibility of losing their jobs if they did not have employer-provided leave or if such leave was insufficient to cover their absences. While family and medical leave benefits in the United States are less generous than those of many other nations[25] (in terms of the length of leave time guaranteed and the fact that it need not be paid), the FMLA guarantees that workers who take

---

[20] *See* 29 U.S.C. §§ 203(*o*), 207, 213.

[21] 29 U.S.C. § 203(g).

[22] 29 C.F.R. § 785.1.

[23] 29 C.F.R. § 785.2 (quoting Skidmore v. Swift & Co., 323 U.S. 134, 138 (1944)).

[24] *See* 29 U.S.C. § 2612.

[25] Much has been written about the lack of paid family and medical leave in the United States as compared with other countries. *See, e.g.*, Christopher Ingraham, *Analysis: The World's Richest Countries Guarantee Mothers More than a Year of Paid Maternity Leave. The U.S. Guarantees Them Nothing*, WASH. POST (Feb. 6, 2018), https://www.washingtonpost.com/news/wonk/wp/2018/02/05/the-worlds-richest-countries-guarantee-mothers-more-than-a-year-of-paid-maternity-leave-the-u-s-guarantees-them-nothing/; Maxine Eichner, *Families, Human Dignity, and State Support for Caretaking: Why the United States' Failure to Ameliorate the Work-Family Conflict is a Dereliction of the Government's Basic Responsibilities*, 88 N.C. L. REV. 1593 (2010).

approved FMLA leave are entitled to return to the same job or an equivalent job. To be equivalent, a job must:[26]

- Offer the same shift or general work schedule, and be at a geographically proximate worksite;

- Involve the same or substantially similar duties, responsibilities, and status;

- Include the same general level of skill, effort, responsibility and authority;

- Offer identical pay, including equivalent premium pay, overtime and bonus opportunities, profit-sharing, or other payments, and any unconditional pay increases that occurred during FMLA leave; and

- Offer identical benefits.

Recognizing that different medical conditions require different treatments, the FMLA's leave policy is flexible. Depending on the circumstances, the leave may be in blocks of time or on an "intermittent" or reduced schedule.[27] This can be particularly important for employees who need regular time off for medical treatments such as chemotherapy, those who experience episodic flareups of serious medical conditions, or those who need a reduced schedule while healing from an injury.[28]

One issue that can be particularly troublesome is whether absences of less than one day must be paid. As a general rule, whether an employer may deduct such time off from an employee's wages usually depends on whether the employee is exempt or non-exempt under the FLSA.[29] Although the wages of non-exempt employees may be reduced for time not "working," it can be dangerous to reduce the salary of exempt employees because the law states:

> An employer who makes improper deductions from salary shall lose the exemption if the facts demonstrate that the employer did not intend to pay employees on a salary basis. An actual practice of making improper deductions demonstrates that the employer did not intend to pay employees on a salary basis.[30]

These rules can change when the leave is FMLA-qualified, and the employer is covered by the FMLA.[31]

Because non-exempt employees are paid on an hourly basis, and only for hours worked, deductions for FMLA-related absences of less than one day are generally permitted under the FLSA for this group of employees. When the time off is for fragments of hours spent on the employer's premises, rather than at home or at a medical appointment, however, the issue becomes more complex.

---

[26]   *See* 29 U.S.C. § 2614; 29 C.F.R. §§ 825.214–.215.

[27]   *See* 29 U.S.C. § 2612(b); 29 C.F.R. § 825.205.

[28]   Although the law does not require that FMLA leave be paid, an employer may require its employees to use available accrued paid leave if the employer provides it. Thus, some or all of the leave may be paid. *See* 29 C.F.R. § 825.207.

[29]   *See* 29 C.F.R. §§ 541.602–.603. Whether time off is properly viewed as compensated "work" can also depend on how long and for what purpose the time-off is taken. In 29 C.F.R § 725, the DOL addresses whether waiting time, rest and meal periods, sleeping time and many other employment-related time is compensable "work" time under the FLSA.

[30]   29 C.F.R. § 541.603(a). *See generally* Jared P. Buckley et al., *Collective Actions Breathe New Life into the Fair Labor Standards Act's Salary Test*, 50 WAYNE L. REV. 905 (2004). *See also, e.g.,* In re Wal-Mart Stores, 395 F.3d 1177 (10th Cir. 2005) (discussing the effect of prospective reductions in pay).

[31]   *See* 29 C.F.R. § 825.206.

Exercise 15: FMLA Eligibility

MEMORANDUM

TO: Labor and Employment Law Associates

FROM: Margaret Willis

DATE: August 15, YR-00

RE: Nirvana Pharm. Inc.—FMLA Leave/FLSA Issue

L & E Associates:

Eva Bennett, the employee benefits manager at Nirvana Pharmaceuticals, has asked whether its employee, Edgar Elliott, is entitled to FMLA leave. Below is a copy of the notes she took of a conversation with Elliott. Nirvana is a new client that originally came to the firm for tax work, so I do not know much about the company. I don't think she provided us with enough information to determine his eligibility. Please provide a list of questions I can ask her because I need to get back to her today. Please refer to 29 U.S.C. § 2601, *et seq.* and 29 C.F.R. § 825 and its subparts. To get a head start, you might also use the DOL's FMLA elaws advisor, or one of its "fact sheets."

Thank you,

MW

Notes of Conversation with Edgar Elliott – August 15, YR-00

Edgar called me quite upset. He fell during the marathon and is at the hospital. He went to the emergency room and is going to an orthopedic specialist today. Apparently, he broke bones. He and another runner collided, and he hit the curb when he fell.

Exercise 16: FMLA and FLSA Compensable Time

MEMORANDUM

TO:	Labor and Employment Law Associates
FROM:	Margaret Willis
DATE:	September 28, YR-00
RE:	Nirvana Pharm. Inc.—FMLA Leave/FLSA Issue

L & E Associates:

Nirvana has asked us to provide a response to a letter it received from an attorney who represents Edgar Elliott regarding Elliott's purported entitlement to paid break time while he recovers from his injury. I assume that the attorney is Elliott's relative.

I have attached the attorney's letter and my draft response. I have also attached documents related to Elliott's FMLA leave. I need you to review his letter and the authority he cites. I also need you to review my draft response and update the law, if necessary. There is some confusion apparently regarding whether Elliott must be paid for his short work breaks under the Fair Labor Standards Act. Has the Dept. of Labor clarified its position on whether the FLSA requires employers to pay employees for short work breaks when those breaks are FMLA-related?

Thank you,

MW

Nirvana Documentation Regarding FMLA Time

REGAN, SEVERSON, & ZHIRI
ATTORNEYS AT LAW
4 FARAWAY EXPRESSWAY
NOTHIN, NT 54321

September 25, YR-00

Eva Bennett
Employee Benefits & Human Resources
Nirvana Pharmaceuticals Inc.
3822 Monticello Ave.
Nothin, NT 54321

Re: FLSA Violation in Regard to Edgar Elliott

Dear Ms. Bennett:

We represent Edgar Elliott regarding the conditions under which he is currently working. As you know, he recovered from his injury such that he was able to return to his job full time as long as he takes 15-minute breaks every hour. His job patrolling the premises is very tiring and can cause him pain. He hopes to recover so those breaks are no longer needed, but he is not there yet.

You have informed him that, because he has exhausted his paid leave, although not his Family and Medical Leave entitlement, his 15-minute breaks are being treated as FMLA time off. Since he is an hourly non-exempt worker, Nirvana is not paying him for his time off. As a result, Mr. Elliott is only being paid for six hours for every eight-hour shift.

Nirvana's failure to pay for Mr. Elliott's break time violates the Fair Labor Standards Act because the break time is compensable. Although the FLSA does not expressly define compensable work time, the applicable regulations state: "Rest periods of short duration, running from 5 minutes to about 20 minutes, are common in industry. They promote the efficiency of the employee and are customarily paid for as working time. They must be counted as hours worked." 29 C.F.R. § 785.18. As noted by the Third Circuit, "The FLSA does not require employers to provide their employees with breaks. However, if an employer chooses to provide short breaks of five to twenty minutes, the employer is required to compensate employees for such breaks as hours worked." *Sec'y of United States DOL v. Am. Future Sys.*, 873 F.3d 420, 430 (3d Cir. 2017).

Mr. Elliott has no interest in interjecting strife into his relationship with Nirvana. He does, however, have an interest in getting paid. If Nirvana refuses to do so, we will have no choice but to get the Department of Labor involved. Please contact me at 555-5858 upon receipt of this letter.

Sincerely yours,

R. Elliott

Roberto Elliott
Attorney
relliott@email.com
cc: E. Elliott

WILLIS, JAMES, MARTIN & PEABODY
ATTORNEYS AT LAW
22 EAGLE BEND DRIVE
NOTHIN, NT 54321

September 28, YR-00

Roberto Elliott
Regan, Severson, & Zhiri
Attorneys at Law
4 Faraway Expressway
Nothin, NT 54321

Re: Edgar Elliott's Rest Breaks

Dear Mr. Elliott:

My firm represents Nirvana Pharmaceuticals, Inc. Ms. Eva Bennett has forwarded your letter of September 25, YR-00 to me for response. In your letter, you allege that Nirvana has violated the Fair Labor Standards Act by failing to pay Mr. Elliott for his hourly 15-minute breaks. The authority you cite is not applicable to the current situation. Although Nirvana recognizes and adheres to the position that break times of five to twenty minutes are normally compensable, that principle recognizes that the employer benefits from having a workforce that has been energized by the break. On the other hand, the law also recognizes that "periods during which an employee is completely relieved from duty and which are long enough to enable him to use the time effectively for his own purposes are not hours worked." 29 C.F.R. § 785.16.

As the Secretary of Labor noted in its brief in *Sec'y of United States DOL v. Am. Future Sys.*, 873 F.3d 420, 430 (3d Cir. 2017), "where an employee requires an accommodation for a medical condition or that entails taking repeated short breaks, it is reasonable to conclude that the accommodation renders the break predominantly for the employee's benefit and therefore non-compensable." *See also Spiteri v. AT&T Holdings, Inc.*, 40 F. Supp. 3d 869 (E.D. Mich. 2014), which the Secretary of Labor cited with approval in *American Future Systems*.

In this case, Mr. Elliott's hourly breaks are predominately for his benefit and he is completely relieved from duty. This renders the time non-compensable.

Should you have any further questions, or if I can provide you with any other information, please feel free to contact me at 555-8585.

Sincerely yours,

Margaret Willis, Esq.
willis@wjmp.com

NIRVANA PHARMACEUTICALS, INC.　　　　　　　**EVA BENNET**

- *Notes of conversation with Edgar Elliott – August 15, YR-00*

Edgar called me quite upset. He fell during the marathon and is at the hospital. He went to the emergency room and is going to an orthopedic specialist today. Apparently, he broke bones. He and another runner collided, and he hit the curb when he fell. Edgar isn't sure when he can come back to work but he knows that he doesn't have much sick leave or vacation time left.

He called back and told me that he would be off of work for at least one week and maybe more. He will need to follow up with his physician. I told him I would mail the FMLA paperwork to him today and that he should return it with the required information as soon as possible.

- *Notes of conversation with Edgar Elliott – August 18, YR-00*

Edgar has a cast on and is undergoing treatment. He got the FMLA paperwork and his doctor will send it in. He still can't come in to work now. He will probably have to be out a while. He sees the doctor again in a week.

- *Notes of conversation with Edgar Elliott – August 27, YR-00*

Edgar will probably have to be out until mid-September. I reminded him not to return until his doctor has cleared him to return. He must submit the return-to-work medical certification form indicating that he has been cleared.

- *Notes of conversation with Edgar Elliott – September 13, YR-00*

Edgar and I talked by phone today so that I could remind him that his paid vacation and sick leave will be used as of 9/16. He understands that his remaining FMLA leave will be unpaid.

Notice of Eligibility and Rights & Responsibilities - Family and Medical Leave Act	Nirvana Pharmaceuticals, Inc. Human Resources

In general, to be eligible for FMLA leave, an employee must have worked for Nirvana for at least 12 months, meet the hours of service requirement in the 12 months preceding the leave, and work at a Nirvana site with at least 50 employees within 75 miles. **Actual eligibility for leave will depend on several different factors that are unique to each employee's particular circumstances. Thus, it is important that all of the information requested be provided.**

[Part A – NOTICE OF ELIGIBILITY]

TO: <u>Edgar Elliott</u>
         Employee

FROM: <u>Eva Bennett</u>
         Employer Representative

DATE: <u>August 15, YR-00</u>

On <u>August 15, YR-00</u>, you informed us that you needed leave beginning on <u>immediately</u> for: <u>(a leg fracture)</u>.

_____   The birth of a child, or placement of a child with you for adoption or foster care;

__X__   Your own serious health condition;

_____   Because you are needed to care for your ___ spouse; ___ child; ___ parent due to his/her serious health condition

_____   Because of a qualifying exigency arising out of the fact that your ___ spouse; ___ son or daughter; ___ parent is on covered active duty or call to covered active duty status with the Armed Forces.

_____   Because you are the ___ spouse; ___ son or daughter; ___ parent; ___ next of kin of a covered servicememeber with a serious injury or illness.

This Notice is to inform you that you:

__X__   Are eligible for FMLA leave (See Part B below for Rights and Responsibilities)

_____   Are **not** eligible for FMLA leave, because (only one reason need be checked, although you may not be eligible for other reasons):

        _____   You have not met the FMLA's 12-month length of service requirement. As of the first date of requested leave, you will have worked approximately ____ months towards this requirement.

        _____   You have not met the FMLA's hours of service requirement.

        _____   You do not work and/or report to a site with 50 or more employees within 75 miles.

If you have any questions, contact <u>Eva Bennett – Nirvana Director of Human Resources and Employee Benefits</u> or view the FMLA poster located in <u>the employee break room next to the microwave oven</u>.

[PART B-RIGHTS AND RESPONSIBILITIES FOR TAKING FMLA LEAVE]

As explained in Part A, you meet the eligibility requirements for taking FMLA leave and still have FMLA leave available in the applicable 12-month period. **However, in order for us to determine whether your absence qualifies as FMLA leave, you must return the following information to us by <u>September 7, YR-00</u>.** (If a certification is requested, employers must allow at least 15 calendar days from receipt of this notice; additional time may be required in some circumstances.) If sufficient information is not provided in a timely manner, your leave may be denied.

CONTINUED ON NEXT PAGE

__X__   Sufficient certification to support your request for FMLA leave. A certification form that sets forth the information necessary to support your request **IS** / ~~is not~~ enclosed.

_____   Sufficient documentation to establish the required relationship between you and your family member.

_____   Other information needed (such as documentation for military family leave): _____

_____

_____

_____   No additional information requested

If your leave does qualify as FMLA leave you will have the following **responsibilities** while on FMLA leave (only checked blanks apply):

__X__   Contact __Eva Bennett__ at _____Employee Benefits 555-2468_____ to make arrangements to continue to make your share of the premium payments on y our health insurance to maintain health benefits while you are on leave. You have a minimum 30-day (<u>or, indicate longer period, if applicable</u>) grace period in which to make premium payments. If payment is not made timely, your group health insurance may be cancelled, provided we notify you in writing at least 15 days before the date that your health coverage will lapse, or, at our option, we may pay your share of the premiums during FMLA leave, and recover these payments from you upon your return to work.

__X__   You will be required to use your available __X__ **paid**, __X__ **sick**, __X__ **vacation**, and/or __X__ **other leave** during your FMLA absence. This means that you will receive your paid leave and the leave will also be considered protected FMLA leave and counted against your FMLA leave entitlement.

_____   Due to your status within the company, you are considered a "key employee" as defined in the FMLA. As a "key employee," restoration to employment may be denied following FMLA leave on the grounds that such restoration will cause substantial and grievous economic injury to us. We **have** / **have not** determined that restoring you to employment at the conclusion of FMLA leave will cause substantial and grievous economic harm to us.

__X__   While on leave you will be required to furnish us with periodic reports of your status and intent to return to work every____ month____ . (<u>Indicate interval of periodic reports, as appropriate for the particular leave situation</u>).

If the circumstances of your leave change, and you are able to return to work earlier than the date indicated on this form, you will be required to notify us at least two workdays prior to the date you intend to report for work.

If your leave does qualify as FMLA leave you will have the following **rights** while on FMLA leave:

- You have a right under the FMLA for up to 12 weeks of unpaid leave in a 12-month period calculated as:

        __X__   the calendar year (January – December). **(You have a total of 48 days of FMLA – qualifying leave left this calendar year)**

        _____   a fixed leave year based on

        _____   the 12-month period measured forward from the date of your first FMLA leave usage.

        _____   a "rolling" 12-month period measured backward from the date of any FMLA leave usage.

- You have a right under the FMLA for up to 26 weeks of unpaid leave in a single 12-month period to care for a covered servicemember with a serious injury or illness. This single 12-month period commenced on _____

- Your health benefits will be maintained during any period of unpaid leave under the same conditions as if you continued to work.

- You must be reinstated to the same or an equivalent job with the same pay, benefits, and terms and conditions of employment on your return from FMLA-protected leave. (If your leave extends beyond the end of your FMLA entitlement, you do not have return rights under FMLA.)

CONTINUED ON NEXT PAGE

- If you do not return to work following FMLA leave for a reason other than: 1) the continuation, recurrence, or onset of a serious health condition which would entitle you to FMLA leave; 2) the continuation, recurrence, or onset of a covered servicemember's serious injury or illness which would entitle you to FMLA leave; or 3) other circumstances beyond your control, you may be required to reimburse us for our share of health insurance premiums paid on your behalf during your FMLA leave.

- If we have not informed you above that you must use accrued paid leave while taking your unpaid FMLA leave entitlement, you have the right to have _____ **sick**, _____ **vacation**, and/or _____ **other leave** run concurrently with your unpaid leave entitlement, provided you meet any applicable requirements of the leave policy. Applicable conditions related to the substitution of paid leave are referenced or set forth below. If you do not meet the requirements for taking paid leave, you remain entitled to take unpaid FMLA leave.

__X__ For a copy of conditions applicable to sick/vacation/other leave usage please refer to E. Bennett available at: 555-2468.

__X__ Applicable conditions for use of paid leave: This is a reminder that you have **20** days remaining of your paid sick leave for this calendar year and **2** days remining for your paid vacation leave because of time you have already used this year. Any remaining FMLA leave to which you are entitled will therefore be unpaid if you require additional FMLA leave after these remaining **22** days of combined accumulated paid leave are taken.

Once we obtain the information from you as specified above, we will inform you, within 5 business days, whether your leave will be designated as FMLA leave and count towards your FMLA leave entitlement. If you have any questions, please do not hesitate to contact:

Eva Bennett _____ at _555-2468_____.

NIRVANA PHARMACEUTICALS

Job Title: Loss Prevention Specialist
Reports To: Store or Warehouse Manager/Risk Management Supervisor
Supervises: None

General Purpose of Position:

Loss Prevention Specialists are responsible for detecting, reporting and resolving matters in the area of inventory shortage, cash handling and theft.

Tasks and Responsibilities:

- Conduct surveillance to detect missing inventory and/or apprehend shoplifters.
- Conduct routine inspections of the facility to maintain and protect assets.
- Assist with the enforcement of company standards as they relate to security and safety procedures.
- Participate in the training of new associates in matters of loss prevention.
- Ensure physical security by monitoring access of associates and visitors.
- Participate in regional and national loss prevention and safety programs.
- Testify on behalf of company in legal proceedings.

Qualifications, Skills and Competencies:

- Bachelor's degree preferred.
- Ability to handle difficult situations with diplomacy.
- Ability to perceive situations accurately.
- Ability to maintain a fair, consistent set of standards, using judgment and discretion.
- Ability to maintain records and documentation.
- Ability to operate all equipment necessary to perform the job.

Requirements:

- Ability to work full time and varied hours/days, including nights, weekends, and holidays, as needed.
- Strong interpersonal, communication, organization and follow-through skills.
- Physical ability to stand and walk for extended periods, and to see or hear activity in the store, and perform all functions as set forth above.

Compensation and Benefits:

- Benefits include 401(k) plan, paid vacation and holidays, and all other benefits enjoyed by Nirvana's full-time associates. Non-Exempt. Pay commensurate with experience.

| Certification of Health Care Provider for Employee's Serious Health Condition - Family and Medical Leave Act | Nirvana Pharmaceuticals, Inc. Human Resources |

To be returned to employee and employer.

SECTION I: For Completion by the EMPLOYER

General Information: The Family and Medical Leave Act (FMLA) provides that an employer may require an employee seeking FMLA protections because of a need for leave due to a serious health condition to submit a medical certification issued by the employee's health care provider. Nirvana will not ask employees to provide more information than allowed under the FMLA regulations, and will maintain records and documents relating to medical certifications, recertifications, or medical histories of employees created for FMLA purposes as confidential medical records in separate files/records from the usual personnel files and in accordance with the FMLA, the Americans with Disabilities Act if it applies, and in accordance with the Genetic Information Nondiscrimination Act, if it applies.

Nirvana contact: __Eva Bennett – Human Resources/Employee Benefits__

Employee's job title: __Loss Prevention Specialist__
Regular Work Schedule: __Full time with nights and weekends, as needed__
Employee's essential job functions: __See attached job description__

Check if job description is attached: ✔

SECTION II: For Completion by the EMPLOYEE

INSTRUCTIONS to the EMPLOYEE: Please complete Section II before giving this form to your medical provider. The FMLA permits an employer to require that you submit a timely, complete, and sufficient medical certification to support a request for FMLA leave due to your own serious health condition. Your response is required to obtain or retain the benefit of FMLA protections. Failure to provide a complete and sufficient medical certification may result in a denial of your FMLA request. As required by the FMLA, Nirvana will give you at least 15 calendar days to return this form.

Your Name: _____ __Edgar__ _____ __Elliott__ _____
                    First   Middle   Last

SECTION III: For Completion by the HEALTH CARE PROVIDER

INSTRUCTIONS to the HEALTH CARE PROVIDER: Your patient has requested leave under the FMLA. Answer, fully and completely, all applicable parts. Several questions seek a response as to the frequency or duration of a condition, treatment, etc. Your answer should be your best estimate based upon your medical knowledge, experience, and examination of the patient. Be as specific as you can; terms such as "lifetime," "unknown," or "indeterminate" may not be sufficient to determine FMLA coverage. Limit your responses to the condition for which the employee is seeking leave. Do not provide information about genetic tests, as defined in 29 C.F.R. § 1635.3(f), genetic services, as defined in 29 C.F.R. § 1635.3(e), or the manifestation of disease or disorder in the employee's family members, 29 C.F.R. § 1635.3(b). Please be sure to sign the form on the last page.

Provider's name and business address: __Andrew Jones__

Type of practice / Medical specialty: __Orthopedic Medicine__

Telephone: __(009) 009-9009__   Fax: ( ) _____

CONTINUED ON NEXT PAGE

PART A: MEDICAL FACTS

1. Approximate date condition commenced: __August 15, YR-00__

   Probable duration of condition: __Approx. 3 months for full healing and normal function__

   Mark below as applicable:

   Was the patient admitted for an overnight stay in a hospital, hospice, or residential medical care facility?

   ___ No ___ Yes. If so, dates of admission: __Treated and released__

   _____

   Date(s) you treated the patient for condition: __August 15, YR-00 and will follow-up periodically__

   _____

   Will the patient need to have treatment visits at least twice per year due to the condition? ___ No ___ Yes

   Was medication, other than over-the-counter medication, prescribed? ___ No _X_ Yes

   Was the patient referred to other health care provider(s) for evaluation or treatment (e.g., physical therapist)?

   ___ No ___ Yes. If so, state the nature of such treatments and expected duration of treatment: __He will require__
   __physical therapy when his cast is removed__

2. Is the medical condition pregnancy? ___ No ___ Yes. If so, expected delivery date: _____

3. Use the information provided by the employer in Section I to answer this question. If the employer fails to provide a list of the employee's essential functions or a job description, answer these questions based upon the employee's own description of his/her job functions.

   Is the employee unable to perform any of his/her job functions due to the condition: _X_ No ___ Yes
   If so, identify the job functions the employee is unable to perform: __He will be out of work for approximately__
   __one month and then will most likely need additional break time but should be able to perform his job duties.__

   _____

4. Describe other relevant medical facts, if any, related to the condition for which the employee seeks leave (such medical facts may include symptoms, diagnosis, or any regimen of continuing treatment such as the use of specialized equipment): __He is currently in a cast and will be in a cast when he returns to work__

   _____

CONTINUED ON NEXT PAGE

PART B: AMOUNT OF LEAVE NEEDED

5. Will the employee be incapacitated for a single continuous period of time due to his/her medical condition, including any time for treatment and recovery? ___ No _X_ Yes

   If so, estimate the beginning and ending dates for the period of incapacity: __8/15/YR-00 – 9/YR-00__

6. Will the employee need to attend follow-up treatment appointments or work part-time or on a reduced schedule because of the employee's medical condition? _X_ No ___ Yes. (additional work breaks may be necessary)

   If so, are the treatments or the reduced number of hours of work medically necessary? ___ No ___ Yes
   Estimate treatment schedule, if any, including the dates of any scheduled appointments and the time required for each appointment, including any recovery period:

   Estimate the part-time or reduced work schedule the employee needs, if any: _____ hour(s) per day; _____ days per week _____ from _____ through _____

7. Will the condition cause episodic flare-ups periodically preventing the employee from performing his/her job functions? _X_ No ___ Yes

   Is it medically necessary for the employee to be absent from work during the flare-ups? ___ No ___ Yes.
   If so, explain: _____
   _____

   Based upon the patient's medical history and your knowledge of the medical condition, estimate the frequency of flare-ups and the duration of related incapacity that the patient may have over the next 6 months (e.g., 1 episode every 3 months lasting 1-2 days):

   Frequency: _____ times per_____week(s)_____month(s)
   Duration: _____ hours or _____ day(s) per episode

ADDITIONAL INFORMATION: IDENTIFY QUESTION NUMBER WITH YOUR ADDITIONAL ANSWER.

Work restrictions will be identified upon his release to work. _____
_____
_____
_____
_____
_____
_____

Andrew Jones   _23 August YR-00_
_____   _____
Signature of Health Care Provider   Date

Designation Notice -
Family and Medical Leave Act

Nirvana Pharmaceuticals, Inc.
Human Resources

Note: Leave covered under the Family and Medical Leave Act (FMLA) will be designated as FMLA-protected and Nirvana will inform employees of the amount of leave that will be counted against the employee's FMLA leave entitlement. In order to determine whether leave is covered under the FMLA, Nirvana reserves the right to have the need for leave be supported by a certification. If the certification is incomplete or insufficient, Nirvana will inform employees in writing what additional information is necessary to make the certification complete and sufficient.

To: **Edgar Elliott**
Date: **August 25, YR-00**

We have reviewed your request for leave under the FMLA and any supporting documentation that you have provided. We received your information on ___**August 24, YR-00**___ and decided:

___✔___   Your FMLA leave request is approved. All leave taken for this reason will be designated as FMLA leave.

The FMLA requires that you notify us as soon as practicable if dates of scheduled leave change or are extended, or were initially unknown. Based on the information you have provided to date, we are providing the following information about the amount of time that will be counted against your leave entitlement:

_____   Provided there is not deviation from your anticipated leave schedule, the following number of hours, days, or weeks will be counted against your leave entitlement: _____

___✔___   Because the leave you will need will be unscheduled, it is not possible to provide the hours, days, or weeks that will be counted against your FMLA entitlement at this time. You have the right to request this information once in a 30-day period (if leave was taken in the 30-day period). **(Your remaining FMLA leave as of 15 August was 48 work days.)**

Please be advised (check if applicable):

_____   You have requested to use paid leave during your FMLA leave. Any paid leave taken for this reason will count against your FMLA leave entitlement.

___✔___   We are requiring you to substitute or use paid leave during your FMLA leave.

___✔___   You will be required to present a fitness-for-duty certificate to be restored to employment. If such certification is not timely received, your return to work may be delayed until certification is provided. A list of the essential functions of your position is ___✔___ is _____ is not attached. If attached, the fitness-for-duty certification must address your ability to perform these functions.

_____   **Additional information is needed to determine if your FMLA leave request can be approved:**

_____   The certification you have provided is not complete and sufficient to determine whether the FMLA applies to your leave request. You must provide the following information no later than _____,
                                                                                      (provide at least seven calendar days)
unless it is not practicable under the particular circumstance despite your diligent good faith efforts, or your leave may be denied. _____
             (Specify information needed to make the certification complete and sufficient)

_____   We are exercising our right to have you obtain a second or third opinion medical certification at our expense, and we will provide further details at a later time.

_____   Your FMLA leave request is Not Approved.
_____   The FMLA does not apply to your leave request
_____   You have exhausted your FMLA leave entitlement in the applicable 12-month period

Return to Work Medical Certification

PART I: To Be Completed by Employee

(Please Print)

1. <u>Edgar</u>   <u>N/A</u>   <u>Elliott</u>
   First Name   Middle Initial   Last Name

2. <u>Loss Prevention Specialist</u>
   Employee's position title

3. <u>August 15, YR-00</u>
   Date leave commenced

4. <u>September 20, 20[-00]</u>
   Date of planned return to work

Edgar Elliott   *September 17, YR-00*
Signature of Employee   Date

PART II: To Be Completed by Employee's Health Care Provider

5. I certify that on *9/20/YR-00*, the named employee is able to resume performing the function of his/her position with or without reasonable accommodation. Necessary accommodation(s) is/are as follows(s):

   Edgar Elliott has some difficulty walking because of his injury and is not capable of a significant amount of standing or walking until further notice. I approve him to work ½ time his first week back and after that he may work full time. Because he tires easily, however, he needs to take one 15-minute rest break for every hour of work. Over-exertion may negatively affect his recovery. I will reevaluate his condition in one month and will modify or continue his accommodation needs at that time.

Dr. Andrew Jones   *September 17, YR-00*
Signature of Health Care Provider   Date

Exercise 17: Wage and Hour Compliance and Return from FMLA Leave

MEMORANDUM

TO: Labor and Employment Law Associates

FROM: Margaret Willis

DATE: October 10, YR-00

RE: Nirvana Pharm. Inc.—FMLA Leave/FLSA Issue

L & E Associates:

Thanks again for your help updating my response to Roberto Elliott regarding Edgar Elliott's FMLA leave. I have attached the letter Elliott sent in reply to that letter. The employee now seeks a transfer to a position that would not require him to take the unpaid hourly breaks during the remainder of this FMLA leave. He suggests that Nirvana should transfer him to the open Risk Management Supervisor position. I have also attached the description for that position and for the other positions that are currently open. I would like your opinion regarding which position would be deemed the most equivalent so that Nirvana may meet its obligations under the FMLA.

Thank you,

MW

REGAN, SEVERSON, & ZHIRI
ATTORNEYS AT LAW
4 FARAWAY EXPRESSWAY
NOTHIN, NT 54321

October 7, YR-00

Margaret Willis
Willis, James, Martin & Peabody
Attorneys at Law
22 Eagle Bend Drive
Nothin, NT 54321

Re: Accommodating Edgar Elliott

Dear Ms. Willis:

Thank you for your prompt response to our September 25 letter to Ms. Bennett. Although the opinion letter does not have the force of law, it is nonetheless important to understand the DOL's position. The situation has become untenable for Mr. Elliott, however. Because his job requires physical stress necessitating frequent rest breaks, and because he is not getting paid for those breaks, he is working part-time instead of full-time.

As you know, the FMLA requires that he be returned to the same job or to an equivalent one per 29 C.F.R. § 825.100. Because the break time should be treated as intermittent leave, Nirvana should transfer him to a position that would better accommodate his current restrictions. See 29 C.F.R. §§ 825.203-.205 .

Because of his previous experience, we believe that Nirvana should immediately transfer him to the open Risk Management Supervisor position. If it would be helpful, we are willing to have a face-to-face meeting with Ms. Bennett and yourself. I am available to meet on Monday, Tuesday, or Friday of the following two weeks. You may also contact me at 555-5858. I look forward to expeditiously resolving this matter.

Sincerely yours,

R. Elliott

Roberto Elliott
Attorney
relliott@email.com
cc: E. Elliott

NIRVANA PHARMACEUTICALS

Job Title: Risk Management Supervisor
Reports To: Vice President of Operations
Supervises: Risk Management Specialists/Loss Prevention Specialists

General Purpose of Position:

The Risk Management Supervisor is responsible for administering and managing Daisy Depot's risk management program.

Tasks and Responsibilities:

- Develops and implements Daisy Depot's risk management program in a manner that fulfills the mission and strategic goals of the organization while complying with state and federal laws.
- Develops and implements systems, policies and procedures for the identification, collection and analysis of risk related information.
- Educates and trains the leadership, staff and business associates as to the risk management program, and their respective responsibilities in carrying out the risk management program.
- Advises departments on designing risk management programs within their own departments.
- Collects, evaluates, and maintains data concerning worker's compensation claims, and other risk-related data.
- Investigates and analyzes root causes, patterns, or trends that could result in compensatory or sentinel events. Helps to identify and implement corrective action where appropriate.
- Provides a quarterly summary to the Vice President of Operations on incidents, claims, and claim payments.
- Serves as the organization's liaison to the organization's insurance carriers.
- Assists in processing summonses and claims against the facility by working with legal counsel to coordinate the investigation, processing, and defense of claims against the organization.
- Actively participates in or facilitates committees related to risk management, safety, and quality improvement.

Qualifications, Skills and Competencies:

- A master's degree in business administration, information technology or similar area preferred.
- Experience in one or more of the following fields: risk management, quality improvement, loss prevention, business administration, legal support or insurance claims investigation, and settlement or patient care.

- Knowledge of statistics, data collection, analysis, and data presentation.
- Excellent interpersonal communication and problem-solving skills.
- Knowledge of federal and state laws and regulations and accreditation standards.

Requirements:

- Ability to work a full-time schedule.
- Retail management experience preferred.
- Availability to travel, as needed.

Compensation and Benefits:

- Benefits include 401(k) plan, paid vacation and holidays, and all other benefits enjoyed by Nirvana's full-time associates. Exempt. Pay commensurate with experience.

NIRVANA PHARMACEUTICALS

Job Title: Customer Service Specialist
Reports To: Store Manager/Customer Service Manager
Supervises: None

General Purpose of Position:

The Customer Service Specialist is responsible for customer satisfaction and customer returns.

Tasks and Responsibilities:

- Perform cashiering tasks as required.
- Be aware of all areas of possible loss due to theft, shoplifting, freebagging, fraud, and/or carelessness and report all such incidents to store management.
- Keep current on all special promotions and sale items and process "rain checks," as necessary.
- Ensure that each customer receives outstanding customer service by providing a friendly environment.
- Authorize and ensure validity of customer returns, exchanges, check authorizations, voids, and discretion discounts.
- Help solve problems that affect the service, efficiency, and productivity of the front end.
- Any other tasks as assigned from time to time.

Qualifications, Skills and Competencies:

- High School degree required. Bachelor's Degree preferred.
- Ability to provide outstanding customer service.
- Ability to adjust priorities and manage time wisely in a fast-paced environment.
- Ability to operate all equipment necessary to perform the job.

Requirements:

- Ability to work a full-time schedule including nights, weekends, and holidays.
- Retail management experience preferred.
- Strong interpersonal, communication, organization and follow-through skills.

Compensation and Benefits:

- Benefits include 401(k) plan, paid vacation and holidays, and all other benefits enjoyed by Nirvana's full-time associates. Non-Exempt. Pay commensurate with experience.

NIRVANA PHARMACEUTICALS

Job Title: Customer Service Manager
Reports To: Store Manager
Supervises: Cashiers

General Purpose of Position:

Working with the Store Manager, the Assistant Store Managers and Department Managers, the Customer Service Manager is responsible for the day-to-day management of the front end, overseeing the cashiers, customer service, and customer returns. Responsibilities include staffing, training, and scheduling of personnel.

Customer Service Managers are also responsible for ensuring the highest level of customer service throughout the store. A Customer Service Manager is a role model and leader and must solve problems, make informed decisions and manage the department wisely in order to achieve maximum results.

Tasks and Responsibilities:

- Assist in the recruitment and hiring of the most qualified applicants to meet the needs of the front end.
- Train, coach and manage all cashiers and customer service personnel in all front-end and relevant company-wide policies and procedures, and conduct monthly customer service audits.
- Supervise and schedule cashiers and customer service personnel and ensure compliance with payroll budgets.
- Be aware of all areas of possible loss due to theft, shoplifting, freebagging, fraud, and/or carelessness.
- Communicate information to front-end personnel regarding special promotions and sale items.
- Expedite front lines, direct flow of customers, and ensure that each customer receives outstanding customer service by providing a friendly environment.
- Work with the operations team to ensure that all transactions that affect the store inventory are processed accurately by auditing the Sales Exception Reports.
- Authorize and ensure validity of customer returns, exchanges, check authorizations, voids, and discretion discounts.
- Oversee compliance of front-end personnel with established Company policies and standards, such as safekeeping of Company funds and property, personnel practices, security, sales and record-keeping procedures.
- Interface with operations to provide orderly maintenance of front-end equipment and supplies.
- Help solve problems that affect the service, efficiency, and productivity of the front end.
- Any other tasks as assigned from time to time.

Qualifications, Skills and Competencies:

- Bachelor's Degree or proven history in customer service with at least three years of experience.
- Ability to provide outstanding customer service.
- Ability to develop and train work force, build relationships and team spirit, utilize skills of workforce most appropriately.
- Ability to manage front end operations effectively.
- Ability to process information/merchandise through computer system and register system.
- Ability to maintain a fair, consistent set of standards as they apply to work force.
- Ability to adjust priorities and manage time wisely in a fast-paced environment.
- Ability to maintain records and documentation pertaining to work force.
- Ability to communicate in a clear, concise, understandable manner, and listen attentively to others, understand material, and provide instructions to all employees.
- Ability to operate all equipment necessary to perform the job.

Requirements:

- Ability to work a full-time schedule including nights, weekends, and holidays.
- Retail management experience preferred.
- Strong interpersonal, communication, organization and follow-through skills.
- Availability to travel, as needed.

Compensation and Benefits:

- Benefits include 401(k) plan, paid vacation and holidays, and all other benefits enjoyed by Nirvana's full-time associates. Exempt. Pay commensurate with experience.

CHAPTER FOUR

INDIVIDUAL EMPLOYMENT RIGHTS

I. INTRODUCTION

The law governing the workplace is derived from several sources—constitutional law, statutory and regulatory law, and common law. Although some employment law issues are controlled by the application of only one of those sources of law, many are not. Without experience, it can be difficult to know whether constitutional law, statutory and regulatory law, or common law—or some combination—control a situation. Moreover, because not all laws affecting the employment relationship are contained in the anti-discrimination or wage and hour laws, it can be very difficult to know whether a state has legislation on discrete issues.

This chapter addresses a few individual rights or "dignitary interests"—such as an employee's rights to information, reputation interests, and privacy interests—that are often rooted in constitutional or common law. Because the research exercises are designed to broaden your understanding of the breadth of state statutory law, they may be situated in states that have codified the specific individual rights addressed in the exercise. In "real life," it might also be necessary to explore constitutional, common-law, and other statutory sources of law to competently advise your clients.

The following research exercises are intended to expose you to state-law topical, or subject-matter-specific, resources. Whether you search "the books" or your library's online resources, look specifically for resources organized by topical area—in this case, employment law or labor and employment law. Topical resources can be quite specific, such as those addressing covenants-not-to-compete, employee privacy, employer eavesdropping, and investigating employee conduct. Becoming familiar with these resources now will increase your competence and confidence later; understanding the breadth and depth of available research resources is critical to your self-evaluation of your research process.

With the increased digitalization of library collections, some libraries have ceased updating the "hard copy" versions of important topical resources. Even in such cases, some libraries have retained the out-of-date versions of resources that are available and current online. Scanning the organizational structure and content of these out-of-date print resources may make using the current online versions easier. Check with your librarian if you are unsure of your access rights to online subject-matter-specific resources.

A. JOB REFERENCES AND ACCESS TO PERSONNEL FILES

As you discovered if you completed Exercise 2, information requested on job applications, medical and psychological tests, and job interviews often provoke tension between an employer's interest in discovering as much as possible about a job applicant and the applicant's rights to limit the information collected. This tension also arises in the context of reference checks: workers seeking new employment hope to receive positive references from former or current employers, new employers hope to obtain truthful references from the sources, and former or current employers hope they will not be sued for any negative statements they make during a reference check. How likely are any of these "hopes" to be fulfilled?

The stakes can be high when a reference check is, or should truthfully be, negative. A current employer may give an undeserved positive reference hoping to rid itself of an unsatisfactory employee or out of concern about the negative effect of a truthful reference on the individual's ability to earn a living. Employers can also be concerned about the possibility of a defamation claim.

These considerations can limit the information obtained during reference checks. Often, the only information that is shared is the employee's job title and dates of employment, which, though helpful, do not give insight into the individual's job performance. And yet, under certain circumstances, a new employer could be exposed to potential common-law liability for negligent hiring if it should have been aware that the new employee posed a significant and unacceptable risk.

Employment lawyers are frequently asked to provide guidance on background checks and employee access to information. To encourage the sharing of truthful, even if negative, job performance information, many states have passed legislation intended to protect the referring employers. Additionally, in some states, employees have express rights to review information maintained in their employment files. Because these measures are often not contained in equal employment opportunity or wage and hour laws, they can be difficult to find. The variety in the scope of the rights provided and in the titles of the statutes, if they do exist, contribute to the difficulty. Using research resources organized by topic can substantially improve the efficiency of research.

Exercise 18:   Job References and Access to Personnel Files

An attorney has contacted Daisy Depot's regional human resources manager claiming to represent a former employee, Emily Emerson, regarding job references the HR manager gave to several companies that were considering hiring Emily. Because she had terminated Emily for a variety of performance-related reasons, she did not give Emily glowing references. In fact, they were rather negative. The attorney is threatening to sue the company on Emily's behalf: he alleges the references were defamatory. Moreover, he asserts that Emily is demanding to see her personnel file and requests immediate access.

Please consider the following questions, analyzing them under the law of the jurisdiction specified by your instructor:

1)   Is Daisy Depot protected by state statutory law with regards to the negative job references she gave to Emily's prospective employers?

2)   Does Emily have any statutory right to see her personnel file under the state law?

B. INDIVIDUAL EMPLOYMENT RIGHTS—PRIVACY

The tension between an employer's need for information and an employee's individual interests can also arise when employers wish to monitor on- and off-the-clock activities of their employees. Common reasons for monitoring on-the-clock activities include: gauging employee efficiency, investigating suspected theft, monitoring compliance with computer-use policies, and ensuring workplace safety.

Although less common, employers might also be interested in their employees' off-the-clock activities, particularly in workplaces with high rates of absenteeism due to illness or injury. While many factors can affect absenteeism—including unsafe working conditions, seasonal illnesses, pregnancy, and other personal circumstances—employers sometimes suspect employees of malingering and abusing the medical leave rights granted to them by the FMLA, workers' compensation laws, and employer-provided leave.[1] Employers sometimes engage in surreptitious measures, such as surveilling or eavesdropping on their employees, to determine whether an employee's need for leave is valid[2] or if leave rights are being abused. In these cases, employers may be constitutionally or statutorily constrained; whether surveillance or eavesdropping occurs at or away from work, employers do not have an unfettered right to invade their employees' legitimate privacy interests.

---

[1] *See, e.g.,* Vail v. Raybestos Prod. Co., 533 F.3d 904 (7th Cir. 2008) (granting summary judgment to employer on an FMLA-interference claim when employer terminated employee after surveillance revealed employee was abusing FMLA leave-of-absence policies).

[2] The FMLA does allow employers to request a second medical opinion (at the employer's expense) if the employer reasonably believes that the certification it received was invalid. 29 U.S.C. § 2613(c) (2012). When there is a conflict between the original and subsequent opinions, the employer may also obtain a third opinion. *See* § 2613(d).

Exercise 19: Privacy

Mona is the employee benefits manager of a large aircraft maintenance facility—Fly Away. Although many such facilities have employee unions, Fly Away does not. One way that the company has avoided unionization over the years has been to treat its employees fairly. For example, the company has generous leave policies. Depending on how long an employee has worked for the company, Fly Away offers employees up to two months of paid personal leave, three months of paid FMLA-qualified leave, and up to two months of unpaid leave for any reason.

Recently, Mona has become concerned with the significant increase in absences relating to illness or injury, especially with those employees who have FMLA-certified intermittent leave. She has noticed that the need for leave disproportionally occurs on Fridays and Mondays. She believes that many employees are malingering, working other jobs, or using paid sick leave instead of paid personal leave or unpaid leave. If that is true, she wants to significantly reduce paid sick leave.

Mona is considering hiring a private investigator to surveil employees who are on extended sick leave or intermittent leave and whom she suspects of malingering. The private investigator would video tape these employees at their home or while they are otherwise not at work to determine whether they are engaged in activities that are inconsistent with their alleged illnesses or injury. Mona is also considering tape recording conversations in the employee break room.

Using any secondary research resources to begin your search, whether online or in your library, please determine whether state statutory law in the jurisdiction identified by your instructor allows the company to audiotape the employees at work or videotape them outside of work if the purpose is to discover whether employees are abusing the company's leave policies. Do not address issues of unlawful surveillance under §§ 7 and 8(a)(1) of the National Labor Relations Act.

II. NON-COMPETITION AGREEMENTS

Companies are increasingly requiring their employees to sign "non-competition" or "non-compete" agreements as a condition of employment. In these agreements, employees are restricted from working for competitors of their employers for a specified period of time after their employment terminates. These agreements often identify the geographic area and the nature of the activities in which the employee is prohibited from working during the specified time period.

These non-competition agreements are controversial. On the one hand, they may serve a legitimate interest in protecting a company's confidential information, which could lose competitive value if it becomes known to others, and in protecting its investment in developing its workforce. On the other hand, non-competes can act as an unnecessary restraint on trade, restricting the ability of individuals to work in a field in which they have trained.

The use of non-competition agreements has become ubiquitous and has expanded beyond occupational sectors that put considerable resources into research and development. In 2014, approximately one-fifth of the U.S. labor force participants were bound by a non-competition agreement,[3] including security guards, camp counselors,[4] and fast-food workers,[5] as examples. Critics note the effect of these agreements on restraining wages and impeding job growth, worker mobility, and entrepreneurship.[6] Some states—California, for example—either refuse to enforce non-competes or limit their use because of the effect they have on restraining trade and worker mobility.

Notwithstanding the criticism, non-competes have been enforced under state statutes and common law if they are designed to protect an employer's "legitimate business interests" and the terms of the agreements are deemed "reasonable." To be reasonable in most states, the limits on the scope of activities workers may perform must be related to the work they performed for their prior employer. Additionally, the geographic boundaries limiting subsequent employment must be reasonably related to the prior employer's area of competition. Finally, the time period in which the employee is constrained must also be reasonable, which may be defined by law or may be dependent on the circumstances of each case. Even if the terms of the non-compete are reasonable, courts may refuse to enforce them if employers require current employees to sign the agreements without providing additional consideration for this important change in the terms and conditions of employment.

Courts approach the validity of non-competition agreements somewhat differently than they do other contracts. Some courts are willing to "blue pencil," or revise, unreasonable terms rather than refusing to enforce them outright.

Employment-law attorneys must always research state law when drafting or reviewing a non-compete. State statutes, when they exist, may have simply codified the common law or they may have abridged it in some way. Multi-volume treatises organized by subject matter or 50-state surveys can make the task of identifying relevant state law easier.

---

[3] Evan Starr, *The Use, Abuse, and Enforceability of Non-Compete and No-Poach Agreements: A Brief Review of the Theory, Evidence, and Recent Reform Efforts*, ECON. INNOVATION GRP. (Feb. 2019), at 2, https://eig.org/wp-content/uploads/2019/02/Non-Competes-Brief.pdf.

[4] Editorial Bd., *Non-Compete Clauses Trap Too Many American Workers*, BLOOMBERG OP. (Nov. 12, 2018), https://www.bloomberg.com/opinion/articles/2018-11-12/non-compete-clauses-trap-too-many-american-workers.

[5] Michael L. Diamond, *State Attorneys General Want to Know More About Fast-Food "No Poach" and Noncompete Agreements*, USA TODAY (July 9, 2018), https://www.usatoday.com/story/money/nation-now/2018/07/09/fast-food-no-poach-agreements/769560002/.

[6] *See Non-Compete Clauses Trap Too Many American Workers*, *supra* note 4.

Exercise 20: Non-Competition Agreements

MEMORANDUM

TO: Labor and Employment Law Associates Assigned to the J & A Team
FROM: Joyce Johnson
DATE: December 3, YR-01
RE: J & A Fabrics: Non-competition Agreement

J & A Team,

Based on the work our firm has done for J & A relating to trade secret misappropriation, it has asked us to assist with a new matter. J & A wants us to draft a non-competition agreement for its employees to sign. The attached letter from J & A's co-owner Adina Addison, provides the parameters of the agreement she would like us to draft.

You should consult York law to determine whether the terms of the agreement J & A wants us to draft are permissible. I have attached the statute for your convenience.

J & A Documentation Regarding Non-Competition Agreement

J & A Fabrics

December 1, YR-01

Joyce M. Johnson
Gould, Rojas, & Johnson
4 Trinity Expressway
Island Park, York 54321

Re: Non-competition Agreements

Dear Ms. Johnson:

Thank you for all of your help suing George Rice and Waring Glen Mills for trade secret misappropriation. I know it's not over, but I am feeling confident that we will prevail and they will be permanently enjoined from using our fabric patterns and secret dye recipes. This case is causing us to evaluate our options. We simply can't have employees going to competitors and giving them our trade secrets. Although confidentiality agreements seemed to work in the past, maybe that's because the workforce was a little older and less mobile. Nowadays, it seems like no one wants to stay at the same job anymore!

Given that, we want you to draft a non-compete agreement that we will have all current and former employees sign. I think it would be fair to ask them not to work for any of our competitors anywhere in the country for at least five years. J & A is well known nationwide and I am sure that there are a lot of companies out there that would love to get our recipes and designs.

I enclose the relevant section of our employee handbook that contains a copy of the current confidentiality agreement we ask our employees to sign. If you have any questions or concerns, please let me know. You know how to reach me. I would like to roll out the non-compete agreements as soon as possible.

Very truly yours,

Adina Addison

J & A Fabrics

Employee Handbook

A Contract between You and J & A Fabrics

About Us

J & A Fabrics has celebrated ten successful years of business. We are a family-owned company run by Jack and Adina Addison and our children Rachel and Ty. We decided to locate our business in Cottonwood Falls, after stopping in town while on a family vacation through the Midwest a few years ago. We had been looking for a peaceful town with a stable and quality workforce and we found it here.

The focus of our enterprise is on transforming raw wool into beautiful and useful fabric. J & A offers custom fabrics to individuals and businesses nationwide. We offer the full spectrum of services involved in natural wool finishing—from the initial processing of raw, unfinished wool to finished shawls, rugs, and furniture fabric. We work with high-quality mohair, which comes from the Angora goat, as well as the wool from Alpacas and Llamas. J & A also stocks silk, soy silk, kid mohair, wool and alpaca to blend with customers' fibers but will also process blends provided by customers.

J & A is also known for the exceptional quality of its custom dyes, which we stew from many natural products, including native and exotic flowers, roots, berries, nuts, insects, and minerals. Versions of this process of dye-making have been around since the first of our ancestors painted on their cave walls. Although amateurs can learn to make homemade dyes via various craft outlets, J & A prides itself on the homemade recipes it uses to create the unique colors we market to our customers.

We also enjoy a considerable reputation for the exceptional quality of our yarn and woven materials. Ty Addison is particularly creative and is therefore responsible for designing finished upholstery patterns. His designs cover the spectrum: from abstract designs based on traditional Persian or Incan motifs to the more traditional tapestries. We are very proud of his designs, several of which have appeared in the Smithsonian. J & A counts among its private clients several very wealthy individuals who "collect" J & A designs and who place regular orders for furniture fabric. The resulting "buzz" has motivated others to order fabrics like those designed for J & A's high-end customers and allowed us to double our workforce in the last 10 years.

Of course, J & A would not be so successful without people like you. We will be counting on you to uphold the quality we are known for and to take pride in your work. We will be counting on you to keep the company secrets that help us produce materials that are the envy of our competitors. Without employees like you, we would not have been able to grow so quickly! We have over 180 workers! With your help, J & A's reputation for quality and originality will persevere.

Welcome to the Team!

J & A Fabrics

Confidentiality Agreement

I, _____ ("Employee"), understand and agree that by working at J & A Fabrics I may learn certain information that is and must be kept confidential. To ensure the protection of such information, and to preserve any confidentiality necessary under patent and/or trade secret law, it is agreed that:

1. The Confidential Information includes:

Proprietary ideas, trade secrets, drawings and/or illustrations, processes and recipes, existing and/or contemplated products, services, and designs, research and development, production, costs, profit and margin information, finances and financial projections, customers, clients, marketing, and current or future business plans and models, regardless of whether such information is designated as "Confidential Information" at the time of its disclosure.

2. The Employee agrees not to disclose the Confidential Information obtained from J & A to anyone unless required to do so by law.

3. This Agreement states the entire agreement between the parties concerning the disclosure of Confidential Information. Any addition or modification to this Agreement must be made in writing and signed by the parties.

4. If any of the provisions of this Agreement are found to be unenforceable, the remainder shall be enforced as fully as possible and the unenforceable provision(s) shall be deemed modified to the limited extent require to permit enforcement of the Agreement as a whole.

WHEREFORE, as a condition of employment with J & A, the Employee acknowledges that he or she has read and understands this Agreement and voluntarily accepts the duties and obligations set forth herein.

Employee Name (Print or Type): _____

Signature: _____

Date: _____

York Statutes Annotated 653.295.

LABOR AND EMPLOYMENT—NON-COMPETE AGREEMENT

(1) A non-competition agreement entered into between an employer and employee is voidable and may not be enforced by a court of this state unless:

    (a)   (A)   The employer informs the employee in a written employment offer received by the employee at least two weeks before the first day of the employee's employment that a non-competition agreement is required as a condition of employment; or

            (B)   The non-competition agreement is entered into upon a subsequent bona fide advancement of the employee by the employer;

    (b)   The employee is a person described in 653.020 (3);

    (c)   The employer has a protectable interest. As used in this paragraph, an employer has a protectable interest when the employee:

        (A)   Has access to trade secrets; or

        (B)   Has access to competitively sensitive confidential business or professional information that otherwise would not qualify as a trade secret, including product development plans, product launch plans, marketing strategy or sales plans; or

        (C)   Is employed as an on-air talent by an employer in the business of broadcasting and the employer:

            (i)   In the year preceding the termination of the employee's employment, expended resources equal to or exceeding 10 percent of the employee's annual salary to develop, improve, train or publicly promote the employee, provided that the resources expended by the employer were expended on media that the employer does not own or control; and

            (ii)   Provides the employee, for the time the employee is restricted from working, the greater of compensation equal to at least 50 percent of the employee's annual gross base salary and commissions at the time of the employee's termination or 50 percent of the median family income for a four-person family, as determined by the United States Census Bureau for the most recent year available at the time of the employee's termination; and

    (d)   The total amount of the employee's annual gross salary and commissions, calculated on an annual basis, at the time of the employee's termination exceeds the median family income for a four-person family, as determined by the United States Census Bureau for the most recent year available at the time of the employee's termination. This paragraph does not apply to an employee described in paragraph (c)(C) of this subsection.; and

    (e)   Within 30 days after the date of the termination of the employee's employment, the employer provides a signed, written copy of the terms of the non-competition agreement to the employee.

(2) The term of a non-competition agreement may not exceed 18 months from the date of the employee's termination. The remainder of a term of a non-competition agreement in excess of 18 months is voidable and may not be enforced by a court of this state.

(3) Subsections (1) and (2) of this section apply only to non-competition agreements made in the context of an employment relationship or contract and not otherwise.

(4) Subsections (1) and (2) of this section do not apply to:

    (a)   Bonus restriction agreements, which are lawful agreements that may be enforced by the courts in this state; or

    (b)   A covenant not to solicit employees of the employer or solicit or transact business with customers of the employer.

(5) Nothing in this section restricts the right of any person to protect trade secrets or other proprietary information by injunction or any other lawful means under other applicable laws.

(6) Notwithstanding subsection (1)(b) and (d) of this section, a non-competition agreement is enforceable for the full term of the agreement, for up to 18 months, if the employer provides the employee, for the time the employee is restricted from working, the greater of:

    (a)   Compensation equal to at least 50 percent of the employee's annual gross base salary and commissions at the time of the employee's termination; or

    (b)   Fifty percent of the median family income for a four-person family, as determined by the United States Census Bureau for the most recent year available at the time of the employee's termination.

(7) As used in this section:

    (a)   "Bonus restriction agreement" means an agreement, written or oral, express or implied, between an employer and employee under which:

        (A)   Competition by the employee with the employer is limited or restrained after termination of employment, but the restraint is limited to a period of time, a geographic area and specified activities, all of which are reasonable in relation to the services described in subparagraph (B) of this paragraph;

        (B)   The services performed by the employee pursuant to the agreement include substantial involvement in management of the employer's business, personal contact with customers, knowledge of customer requirements related to the employer's business or knowledge of trade secrets or other proprietary information of the employer; and

        (C)   The penalty imposed on the employee for competition against the employer is limited to forfeiture of profit sharing or other bonus compensation that has not yet been paid to the employee.

    (b)   "Broadcasting" means the activity of transmitting of any one-way electronic signal by radio waves, microwaves, wires, coaxial cables, wave guides or other conduits of communications.

    (c)   "Employee" and "employer" have the meanings given those terms in 652.310.

    (d)   "Non-competition agreement" means an agreement, written or oral, express or implied, between an employer and employee under which the employee agrees that the employee, either alone or as an employee of another person, will not compete with the employer in providing products, processes or services that are similar to the employer's products, processes or services for a period of time or within a specified geographic area after termination of employment.

CHAPTER FIVE

TERMINATING THE EMPLOYMENT RELATIONSHIP: GROUP TERMINATIONS AND PLANT CLOSINGS

I. INTRODUCTION

The ability to terminate the employment relationship is the ultimate exercise of power in the workplace. Employment law courses are quick to emphasize the primary principles that (1) the relationship between employer and employee is essentially contractual, and (2) it is presumptively terminable at will by either party, with or without notice.

Workers have no legal constraints on their ability to leave their jobs, although they may face consequences if they leave in breach of a term contract. Despite the presumption of at-will employment, however, employers do not have an unfettered power to fire their workers;[1] they may be constrained by common-law rules governing express or implied contracts, public policy, or federal and state constitutions and statutes that prohibit discrimination and retaliation or that provide limited due-process rights. Despite this apparent imbalance, workers often feel they are the more vulnerable party.

Although no legal doctrine interferes with their discretion to direct capital, and employers are generally free to determine the size of their workplace and hire and fire at will, group employee layoffs or plant closings raise the stakes for all involved. A variety of factors can compel a company to shut its doors or reduce its workforce,[2] including economic downturns resulting in decreased demand for a company's goods or services, eliminating unprofitable business units, and seeking a more favorable business climate for the company to operate in. It is not unusual to read news of plant closings or mass layoffs, even when the economy is prospering.

Regardless of the reason for the plant closing or layoff, losing a job under such circumstances can have significant consequences for employees who must now compete with their former coworkers for new positions—a task made even harder in communities without a large or diverse occupational base. Group termination actions can also traumatize the remaining workforce, cause customers and suppliers to seek other vendors or clients, and otherwise counteract the underlying goals of the action,[3] if handled without sensitivity and care. Thus, these large-scale company actions can harm not only the individual employees, but entire communities.

Closing a work site or reducing the workforce requires careful planning. A reduction in force requires careful evaluation of long-term strategic goals and identifying the employees who are necessary to achieve those goals. This often necessitates discharging many excellent employees who may choose not to be rehired if the opportunity arises. The difficult choice of whom to let go should

---

[1] In 1991, the National Conference of Commissioners on Uniform State Laws approved a Model Termination Act that would have prohibited terminating certain qualified employees without "good cause." Although the Commissioners recommended that it be enacted in all of the states, it has received little traction to date. Montana and Puerto Rico do have statutory exceptions to the at-will employment rule. *See* Montana's Wrongful Discharge from Employment Act, MONT. CODE ANN. §§ 39–2–901 to –915 (2017), and Puerto Rico's Indemnity for Discharge without Just Cause, P.R. LAWS ANN. 29 §§ 185a–185m (LEXIS through 2011 Legis. Sess.).

[2] A reduction in force (RIF) is also sometimes called a "downsizing," "rightsizing," "restructuring," or "reorganization." Although the terms "reduction in force," "downsizing," and "layoff" are often used synonymously, a layoff is often seen as a temporary workforce reduction, with affected employees potentially eligible for rehire, while a downsizing is often a permanent workforce reduction.

[3] *See generally* Kenneth W. Freeman, *The Right Way to Close an Operation*, HARV. BUS. REV. (May 2009), https://hbr.org/2009/05/the-right-way-to-close-an-operation.

be based on objective factors and the company should ensure that the selection criteria will not disproportionally affect employees on the basis of race, sex, disability, age or other protected status.

The Bureau of Labor Statistics (BLS) publishes useful information regarding employment trends. Although it eliminated its data collection under the Mass Layoff Statistics program in 2013,[4] it still publishes information regarding mass layoffs. In August 2018, for example, it released a report regarding worker displacement between 2015 and 2017.[5] It found that 3.0 million workers were displaced from jobs they had held for at least three years during that period.[6] Although that number appears high, it is less than half of the 6.9 million workers displaced during the January 2007 to December 2009 recessionary period.[7]

The devastating impact of a job loss tends to be greater for older workers. For example, in its Worker Displacement report for 2015 through 2017, the BLS reported that the reemployment rate for workers aged fifty-five to sixty-four was 60 percent compared with the rate for workers aged sixty-five or older, which was 31 percent.[8] Workers aged twenty-five to fifty-four, on the other hand, had a 76 percent reemployment rate.[9]

In the aftermath of the 2007 to 2009 recession, when the unemployment rate was high, the reemployment rates were lower for all displaced workers but more significantly so for older workers. In its 2018 report, the BLS reported reemployment rates for workers aged twenty to twenty-four to be 55 percent in contrast to the 39 percent rate for workers aged fifty-five to sixty-four.[10] For workers who were sixty-five and older, the reemployment rate was a mere 23 percent.[11]

Federal and state laws provide safety nets for many workers who lose their jobs. Regardless of whether they are terminated individually or as part of a group, federal or state law may entitle them to pension benefits, continued health-care coverage, unemployment compensation, or payment for earned but unused vacation time. A work-site closure or reduction in force may entitle affected employees to additional protections under federal, and in some cases, state law depending on the size of the employer and the number of employees being terminated. For the purposes of this chapter, the most significant of these laws are the Older Workers Benefit Protection Act of 1990 (OWBPA),[12] which amended the Age Discrimination in Employment Act of 1967 (ADEA),[13] and the Worker Adjustment and Retraining Notification Act (WARN)[14] and its state counterparts.

---

[4]   The Bureau of Labor Statistics Mass Layoff Statistics Program identified, described, and tracked the effects of major job cutbacks in the economy. *See Mass Layoff Statistics*, BUREAU OF LABOR STATS., https://www.bls.gov/mls/ (last visited July 1, 2019).

[5]   The BLS defined "displaced workers" as "persons 20 years of age and over who lost or left jobs because their plant or company closed or moved, there was insufficient work for them to do, or their position or shift was abolished." *2015–2017 Worker Displacement*, BUREAU OF LABOR STATS. (Aug. 28, 2018, 10:00 AM), https://www.bls.gov/news.release/archives/disp_08282018.pdf (hereinafter BLS Report 2018).

[6]   *Id.*

[7]   *2007–2009 Worker Displacement*, BUREAU OF LABOR STATS. (Aug. 26, 2010, 10:00 AM), https://www.bls.gov/news.release/archives/disp_08262010.pdf (hereinafter BLS Report 2010).

[8]   BLS Report 2018 at 2.

[9]   *Id.*

[10]   BLS Report 2010 at 2. Age discrimination in hiring accounts for some of these discrepancies. *See, e.g.,* Patricia Cohen, *New Evidence of Age Bias in Hiring and a Push to Fight It*, N.Y. TIMES (June 7, 2019), https://www.nytimes.com/2019/06/07/business/economy/age-discrimination-jobs-hiring.html (reporting on statistical and anecdotal evidence of age discrimination and the ways in which social media platforms contribute to the problem).

[11]   *Id.*

[12]   Older Workers Benefit Protection Act of 1990, Pub. L. No. 101–433, 104 Stat. 978.

[13]   29 U.S.C. §§ 621–31 (2012).

[14]   29 U.S.C. § 2101, *et seq.*

II. SEVERANCE AGREEMENTS AND THE OLDER WORKERS BENEFIT PROTECTION ACT

Before undertaking a layoff or downsizing, some companies embark on an "early retirement incentive program" (ERIP). As its name suggests, an ERIP provides a defined group of employees with the opportunity to leave voluntarily in exchange for benefits to which they would not otherwise be entitled. In many cases, the employees selected are already eligible for retirement benefits and the ERIP is offered to induce them to retire before they otherwise would have intended. To ease the transition and lessen the impact of unemployment, incentives often include salary continuation and "outplacement" services designed to assist the employees in finding replacement employment.

To obtain the benefits of the ERIP or prior to a downsizing, affected employees are often required to sign a severance agreement articulating the special benefits the company will provide upon termination. These severance agreements will contain a waiver and release of potential statutory and common-law claims against the company. Although the enforceability of severance agreements is often determined by the common law, the OWBPA addresses the enforceability of severance agreements accompanying an individual employee's termination,[15] a downsizing, or an ERIP with respect to rights, and the waiver of such rights, under the ADEA.[16]

To be enforceable under the OWBPA, a waiver of ADEA rights or claims must meet the specific criteria regarding content and timing codified at 29 U.S.C. § 626(f). While the content requirements are similar regardless of whether one or more employees are involved, the OWBPA imposes additional requirements when a waiver of age discrimination claims is requested in connection with an exit incentive or other group termination program.

Because of the inherent stress accompanying a downsizing or plant closing, even knowledgeable decision-makers may overlook OWBPA requirements. They may fail to provide information regarding the titles and ages of individuals being discharged, for example, or fail to provide the employee the requisite consideration or rescission periods.[17] They may, in fact, feel pressure to move more quickly than the law allows. It is therefore incumbent on the employer's counsel to ensure the enforceability of any severance agreement and waiver that employees are asked to sign.

---

[15] It is important to note that the OWBPA is relevant whenever an individual is asked to sign a waiver of rights under the ADEA. This includes waivers contained in individual settlement agreements, regardless of whether an age discrimination charge has been raised, if the parties involved are covered by the Act. When drafting or reviewing any agreement settling an employee's claims, the employer's counsel must ensure that all of the OWBPA content and timing requirements are clearly set out.

[16] 29 U.S.C. § 626(f).

[17] *See id.*

Exercise 21: Severance Agreements

MEMORANDUM

TO: Labor and Employment Law Associates Assigned to the J & A Team

FROM: Joyce Johnson

DATE: May 3, YR-00

RE: J & A Fabrics: Reduction in Force

J & A Team,

Unfortunately, J & A downsized its workforce without first seeking our advice. Apparently, one of the laid-off employees is threatening to sue for age discrimination. He signed a severance agreement, which contained a waiver of all potential claims in exchange for eight weeks of severance pay. A copy of his signed agreement is attached. I have also attached a copy of the letter Adina Addison sent me and the letter J & A sent its employees announcing the layoff.

Please review the attached documents and let me know by the end of the week whether J & A's severance agreement and waiver of claims is enforceable against a former employee who now claims age discrimination.

J & A Documents Regarding Its Severance Agreements

May 1, YR-00

Joyce M. Johnson
Gould, Rojas, & Johnson
4 Trinity Expressway
Island Park, York 54321

Re: Discrimination Charge

Dear Ms. Johnson:

As you know, we had to lay off some employees—about 50 of our 180 employees, in fact. The litigation involving the misappropriation of our trade secrets by Waring Glen Mills really hit us hard in many ways, including significant loss of customers. From a financial point of view, we just didn't have the business to justify our large workforce.

We gave all employees whom we laid off eight weeks of severance in exchange for an agreement not to sue us. I revised a form I found online. Given how close we have always been with our employees, and the fact that we didn't think we were doing anything that would subject us to a lawsuit, I thought I could handle it in-house. We were trying to keep our legal expenses under control but maybe we should have asked your opinion ahead of time.

A former employee, Fabian Elmore, is apparently stirring up trouble. He is telling anyone who will listen that we were motivated by age discrimination when we laid off our employees. I don't understand it. Fabian has worked for J & A from the beginning. We really liked him, and I think we treated him well.

Fabian signed the agreement, as you can see from the attached copy of his agreement, so we gave him what we gave everyone else. Now, even though he promised not to sue us, he is threatening to charge us with age discrimination. I don't know why he would think that his age had anything to do with his layoff. He didn't even give us back the severance pay. I have also enclosed the notice we sent out employees when we announced the layoff. Please contact me as soon as you get this.

    Very truly yours,

    Adina Addison

Enc.

J & A Fabrics

April 6, YR-00

Dear J & A Fabrics Employees,

As you know, J & A Fabrics has been experiencing a significant loss of sales due to direct competition by Waring Glen Mills. Waring Glen Mills has replicated some of our signature patterns and dye formulas to make copycat products, which it has been selling at low costs. This has decreased the value of our own products, even though our products are of a much higher quality, and has resulted in a loss of sales. The cost of trying to stop Waring Glen Mills has been significant, in terms of dollars spent on legal fees and in terms of the time and psychological impact of litigation. However, we will continue to fight to save our company!

Although J & A Fabrics has done its best to keep all employees employed during this period, the slowdown has turned out to be longer and more severe than we anticipated. We have finally reached the point where we have no choice but to lay off employees if we want to continue operations. We have therefore decided to downsize our operations. We know how difficult this will be for those whom we are forced to lay off, as well as those who remain. After all, we are a family and we appreciate your efforts in growing the company while maintaining the quality and originality for which we are known.

J & A Fabrics has therefore decided to lay off 50 of our 180 employees, which we will choose from all areas of this plant. We will contact all affected employees this week and they will be offered a severance package as a sign of our esteem and appreciation. Remaining employees will be asked to work a little harder, but we believe that the decrease in customer orders will offset the smaller workforce. We hope that we will win our lawsuit against Waring Glen Mills soon and be able to get our company back on track. We seek your cooperation during this difficult time.

If you have any questions at all about the layoff or the future of J & A Fabrics, please contact one of us.

Best Wishes,

Jack, Adina, Rachel, and Ty

J & A Fabrics

Severance Agreement and Waiver of Claims

This Agreement is entered into between J & A Fabrics, Inc. ("J & A") and Fabian Elmore ("Employee") on this 12th day of April, YR-00. J & A and Employee agree that J & A will provide eight weeks of severance pay to Employee, at the same rate at which Employee currently earns. Employee expressly agrees that Employee is not otherwise entitled to severance pay.

Additionally, J & A will continue to pay its share of Employee's health insurance costs under the same terms as during Employee's employment for eight weeks, after which time, as provided by the Consolidated Omnibus Budget Reconciliation Act of 1985 (COBRA), Employee has a right to elect continued coverage under J & A's group health plan, at his or her own expense, for a period of eighteen months from the date of this release. Such election must be made no later than sixty days after that date.

J & A will provide Employee with job references and other assistance to secure new employment to the extent possible, including up to $1000 in outplacement services.

In consideration for the severance pay and other benefits referred to above, Employee agrees to waive and release all claims and potential claims arising from Employee's employment at J & A, and the termination of Employee's employment, currently known or unknown, excluding any claim to Worker's Compensation or Unemployment Compensation. Employee may seek the advice of an attorney before executing this Agreement.

Employee will return to J & A any confidential proprietary company information he/she possesses and will not reveal any confidential proprietary company learned during his/her tenure at the company to any other person or entity.

This agreement shall not be construed as an admission by J & A that it has engaged in any acts of wrongdoing against Employee or any other person.

J & A Fabrics, Inc. by: __Jack Addison, President__   Employee: _Fabian Elmore_

III. PLANT CLOSING AND LAYOFFS: THE IMPORTANCE OF NOTICE

Because of the hardship that a large-scale reduction in force or a company closing can have on employees and the communities in which they live, the Worker Adjustment and Retraining Notification (WARN) Act[18] requires employers with 100 or more employees to provide sixty days' notice of a covered layoff or plant closing to employees or their representatives, as well as to the chief elected official, such as the mayor, where the employment site is located, and to the "state dislocated worker unit rapid response coordinators." The WARN Act also applies if all or part of a business is sold.

The notice requirement allows affected employees and their families time to plan for the job loss and find alternative employment, if possible. It also provides an opportunity for state and local governments to marshal resources to assist workers in finding jobs or to re-train them for new jobs, if necessary.

The Department of Labor administers the WARN Act. Its website provides compliance assistance for workers and employers, including guides, fact sheets, and contact information for state rapid response coordinators. The DOL has no enforcement power, however. If a company fails to give the required notice, employees or their representatives, such as unions, and local governmental units may bring individual or class actions against the employer in federal district courts.

Some states have their own WARN Acts. As in the case of other employment laws, some of those state laws largely mirror federal law; others provide additional benefits. Maine, for example, requires covered employers to pay eligible employees severance pay in the amount of one week's pay for each year of employment, unless a statutory exception applies.[19]

In many cases, the factors that would trigger the WARN Act's notice requirements are well known ahead of time; the sale of all or part of a business, increased competition, or decreased demand for products or services, for example. In such cases, an employer can take the time to carefully plan and implement the downsizing or closing and protect itself and its employees against the negative consequences that necessarily flow from large-scale employment losses.

In other cases, the causes may be more sudden or unpredictable. In the last few years, the United States has witnessed the significant economic impact of sudden weather-related events such as hurricanes and wildfires. The effect of abrupt changes in national trade policy have also been difficult to predict, with some industrial sectors growing and others retracting during recent trade wars.[20]

To allow necessary flexibility in these circumstances, the Act allows for exceptions to the sixty-day notice requirement when layoffs and closures are due to unforeseen circumstances, faltering companies, and natural disasters.[21] Even in the case of natural disasters, however, it can be difficult to determine when the exceptions apply. For example, the regulations distinguish between mass

---

[18]   29 U.S.C. §§ 2101–2109; 20 C.F.R. § 639 (2018).

[19]   ME. REV. STAT. tit. 26, § 625–B (2018).

[20]   Although the Trump administration's trade tariffs have resulted in some job gains, they have also resulted in company downsizing and closings. *See, e.g.,* Heather Long, *The First Layoffs from Trump's Tariffs are Here,* WASH. POST (June 25, 2018), https://www.washingtonpost.com/news/wonk/wp/2018/06/25/the-first-layoffs-from-trumps-tariffs-are-here/ (reporting on job gains and losses); Jeffrey Kucik, *Trump Tariffs: How the Trade Wars are Affecting Manufacturing Jobs and Pay,* MARKET WATCH (May 17, 2019), https://www.marketwatch.com/story/trump-tariffs-how-the-trade-wars-are-affecting-manufacturing-jobs-and-pay-2019-05-17 (reporting on the uneven impact of tariffs across industrial sectors); Joe Deaux, *U.S. Beer Industry Blames Trump Tariffs for 40,000 Job Losses,* BLOOMBERG (May 23, 2019), https://www.bloomberg.com/news/articles/2019-05-23/u-s-beer-industry-blames-trump-tariffs-for-u-s-jobs-decline (reporting on the effects of aluminum tariffs).

[21]   *See* 29 U.S.C. § 2102(b); 20 C.F.R. § 639.9.

layoffs and plant closings that are the direct or indirect result of natural disasters[22] and whether a layoff or shutdown is "foreseeable" is often a question of fact.[23] Because of the significant penalties involved if a company fails to give the required notice,[24] attorneys advising companies must exercise caution and due diligence before determining that an exception applies.

---

[22] 20 C.F.R. § 639.9(c).

[23] *See, e.g.,* Pena v. Am. Meat Packing Corp., 362 F.3d 418 (7th Cir. 2004).

[24] 29 U.S.C. § 2104.

Exercise 22:   Final Notice

MEMORANDUM

TO: Labor and Employment Law Associates Assigned to the J & A Team

FROM: Joyce Johnson

DATE: August 7, YR-00

RE: J & A Fabrics: Closing

J & A Team,

Thanks for your assistance advising J & A on the issues raised with its severance agreement. The layoff did not have the hoped-for effect of giving J & A the opportunity to stabilize its operations and, despite its troubles with Waring Glen Mills, J & A entered into negotiations to sell the business to Waring Glen Mills. Unfortunately, those negotiations failed.

J & A has decided to shut down. Jack and Adina are ready to retire, and Rachel and Ty are ready to move on. Our corporate department will assist J & A in winding down the company, but it has asked us to help them with notifying its employees.

J & A has already provided conditional notice that it might close but has not sent the final notice. After the trouble it had under the OWBPA when executing its layoff, the company wants to ensure that it is complying with the WARN Act.

Please review the following correspondence. The first letter announced the possibility that it might close, the second announced that it was negotiating with Waring Glen Mills to sell it the business, and the third is a letter J & A would like to send out this week if possible.

Please review the WARN Act and its regulations. You should first double check whether J & A is still covered by WARN. If it is, you should determine whether it would potentially violate WARN if the notice was sent this week. If so, do any of the three exceptions apply?

I gave a presentation on WARN several months ago. Since I only included main points on the slides and presented the nuances and details orally, it doesn't include everything you need to know. Nevertheless, I thought it might give you a head start.

J & A Notices Regarding Plant Closing

J & A Fabrics

June 4, YR-00

Dear J & A Fabrics Employees,

We know that the last two months have been very difficult for you as we had to lay off employees and downsize our operations. We took those steps to ensure the future of the company. Unfortunately, it may not have been enough.

We are considering our options and may choose to narrow the scope of our operations further. We may focus more on design and less on production. We plan to make that decision within the next month but want to give you notice now that we may decide to shut down our operations entirely rather than go forward on a limited basis. This is not a step we would undertake lightly. The company has been our pride and joy and we view all of you as part of our extended family.

If you choose to leave now, we will understand, although we will be unhappy to see you go. Those who choose to go within the next two weeks will receive one month of severance pay as a token of our esteem. We will assess our situation daily. Please let us know if you have any questions. We seek your cooperation during this difficult time.

Please remember that your confidentiality and non-competition agreements remain in effect regardless of the circumstances of your separation from the company.

Best Wishes,

Jack, Adina, Rachel, and Ty

J & A Fabrics

June 18, YR-00

Dear J & A Fabrics Employees,

In our notice to you on June 4, we advised you that we were considering our options, including the possibility that we might have to shut down our operations. Since then, we have lost an additional 10 employees who have chosen to work elsewhere. We wish them the best.

For those of you who remain, we are happy to say that we have begun discussions with Waring Glen Mills to sell it our business, including our recipes, processes, and designs. If we can come to favorable terms, which include a provision that the company maintain your employment for at least six months, we will let you know. If not, we are likely to close immediately.

Please remember that your confidentiality and non-competition agreements remain in effect. Please let us know if you have any questions.

Jack, Adina, Rachel, and Ty

J & A Fabrics

August 12, YR-00   *Is this sufficient notice under WARN in light of the previous communications with J & A employees?*

Dear J & A Fabrics employees,

In our notice of June 18, we announced that we had entered into discussions with Waring Glen Mills to sell our business. We are sorry to say that the negotiations have failed. Given that, we have made the hard decision to close our operations entirely. After the hectic pace of creating and growing such a creative business, we all feel that we need a break and time to consider our options for the future.

We will begin the process of winding down our operations immediately. We will do everything within our power to assist you in the future.

Please let us know if you have any questions. Please remember that your confidentiality and non-competition agreements remain in effect. We seek your cooperation during this difficult time.

Jack, Adina, Rachel, and Ty

The Worker Adjustment and Retraining Notification Act

Gould, Rojas, & Johnson
MAY YR-00

A SUMMARY OF YOUR OBLIGATIONS TO PROVIDE
ADVANCE NOTICE OF CLOSINGS AND LAYOFFS
UNDER WARN

A General
Summary

As an employer, you are required to give your employees 60 days advance notice of a covered plant closing or layoff. This notice must be provided to affected workers or their labor representatives; to the State dislocated worker unit; and to the appropriate unit of local government.

You are covered by WARN if you have 100 or more employees, not including certain part-time employees or recent hires, but including hourly, salaried, managerial, and supervisory employees.

The notice requirements of WARN are triggered if you are shutting down an employment site (or one or more facilities or operating units within such a site), and 50 or more employees will lose their job during any 30-day period.

You are also required to give notice if you engage in a mass layoff that will result in job losses during any 30-day period for 500 or more employees, or for 50-499 employees if they make up at least 33% of your workforce.

The sale of part or all of a business also triggers notice requirements.

Exemptions and Exceptions

WARN does not require you to give notice if the plant being closed is a temporary facility, or if the layoff or closing results from the termination of a particular project, if employees are hired with the understanding that the duration of their employment is limited.

You don't have to provide notice to strikers under certain circumstances but employees who are not part of the bargaining unit engaged in negotiations that lead to a lockout are still entitled to notice.

WARN contains three exceptions to the 60-day notice requirement:

1) Faltering company;
2) Unforeseeable business circumstances: and
3) Natural Disaster.

If one of these exceptions apply, you must still provide as much notice as practicable and the notices must provide a brief statement of the reason for the reduced notice period in addition to other required content.

Form and Content

Although no particular form of notice is required, all notices must be in writing. Any reasonable method of delivery is acceptable as long as employees will receive the notice 60 days before the closing or layoff.

The notice must be specific. You can give conditional notice upon the occurrence or non-occurrence of an event only if the event is definite and its occurrence or non-occurrence will result in a covered employment action less than 60 days after the event.

More information about the content of notices can be found in 20 C.F.R. § 639.7.

The penalties for covered employers who fail to provide appropriate and timely notice can be significant. You might owe every employee who should have received notice back pay and benefits for the violation period, up to 60 days.

You could also be subject to a civil penalty of up to $500 for each day of the violation.

Don't let this be you!

Call Gould, Rojas, & Johnson at 444-3333
BEFORE
you conduct a layoff or shut your doors!
We will help you write your notices, create enforceable severance agreements, and contact the appropriate state government personnel.

For more information on the WARN Act and its regulations, see
29 U.S.C. §§ 2101-2109 and 20 C.F.R. § 639

The text of this presentation is taken from the United States Department of Labor's WARN Fact Sheet, which can be located at:
https://www.dol.gov/general/topic/termination/plantclosings